Extra! Extra!

THE ORPHAN TRAINS

and

Newsboys of

New York

by

RENÉE WENDINGER

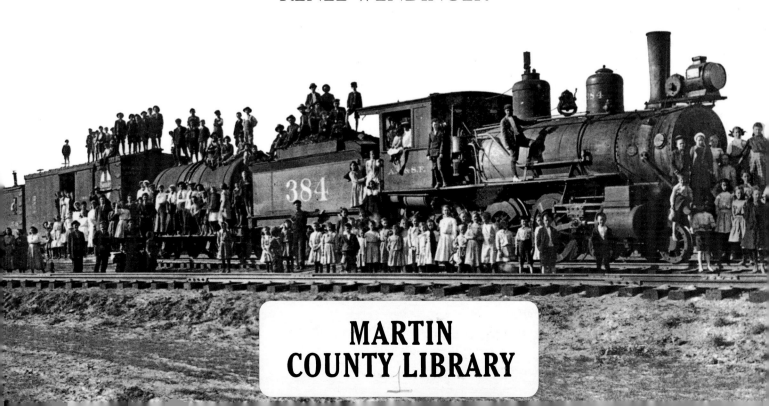

ACKNOWLEDGEMENTS

I extend an immense thank-you to the New York Children's Aid Society and the New York Foundling Hospital for archival history and pictures. Likewise, my deep appreciation turns to the Library of Congress for photos from the Prints and Photographs Division Online Catalog of the National Child Labor Committee Collection (e.g. LC-USZ62-108765) as unrestricted use of the Lewis Wickes Hine child labor photographs commencing from a government organization source. My thanks as well to the George Eastman House for the exceptional photographs captured by Lewis Wickes Hine and to the Museum of the City of New York for the astounding photographs from Jacob Riis. These two men had the prudence to record history through skilled photography and journalistic insight.

Comparably, I'd like to express an extensive thank-you to The New York Times newspaper archives for use of published commentaries prior to 1923 and to the Minnesota Historical Society Division of Newspaper Research. Thank you Mount Loretto, Staten Island, for Father John Drumgoole chronicles. An important thank-you is extended to the Kansas Historical Society for utilization of an authentic orphan train picture.

Gratitude is expressed to actress 'Baby Peggy' Jean Montgomery (Diana Serra Cary) for communicating with me about her opportunistic meeting with the New York Foundling Hospital orphans and disclosed film.

I would like to extend a heartfelt thank-you to the Midwest Orphan Train Riders from New York and their descendants for providing personal histories and photographs to this reserve. I couldn't have done it without you!

I would like to express thanks to Pennefeather Editorial Services in St. Paul, Minnesota for constructive editing proficiency.

Last, but certainly never least, substantiated merit is extended to my husband, Lonnie, for his patience so I could place this writing. To Patty, Char, Jonni, and Steve, my extraordinary siblings, for their dependable and supportive encouragement motivated by a common bond, our mother, Sophia Hillesheim, 1917 New York Orphan Train Rider to Minnesota.

Extra! Extra!
The Orphan Trains and
Newsboys of New York
by Renée Wendinger

First Printing: October 2009
ISBN: 978-0-615-30930-9
Library of Congress Control Number: 2009932586

Published by:
Legendary Publications
PO Box 482
Sleepy Eye, Minnesota 56085
Website: http://www.theorphantrain.com
Printed in the United States of America
Cover design by Renée Wendinger
Cover photo courtesy of the Kansas Historical Society and the Library of Congress.

Preface

In view of the fact that there are currently six arranged volumes of Orphan Train Riders, Their Own Stories, I have not included a full biography of the Orphan Train Riders represented in this book. Instead I chose to impress upon a narrative portrait through exemplary image representation necessary for authentic accuracy. Many of the orphan train riders either possessed very few photographs of themselves as a child, and for others pictures were non-existent. The portraits in this book, though scanty, are fundamentally represented as provided.

I was inspired to gather newsworthy commentaries and arrange them to effectively communicate little-known details about the composition of the orphan trains that departed New York City carrying children from various East Coast orphanages. These children were dispatched west throughout the years 1854-1929 in favor of realizing a new family home. Orphaned and fostered children from other orphanages throughout the United States arriving by train to various towns and family homes were neither affiliated with the orphan trains nor a part of their history.

I elected to complement this story with anecdotal history about the newsboys of New York who were profoundly connected with the orphan trains. The newsies, as they were often called, possessed an amusing persona, were frequently poignant, and were oftentimes inspiring.

My expectations are that you, the reader, will find this book an interesting, enjoyable, and educational element of historical literature. This book preserves a little-known piece of American History.

A 1904 orphan train departing for Texas.

The Children's Aid Society Collection

Dedication

A very loving thank-you
goes to my mother
Sophia (Kaminsky) Hillesheim
who inspired me!

"There are only two lasting bequests
we can hope to give our children.
One is roots; the other, wings."

Hodding Carter

(journalist, writer)

CONTENTS

PART I

⁓

THE ORPHAN TRAINS

Ready to be sent west, this company of boys stand in front of the Children's Aid Society office at 105 East 22nd Street.

The Children's Aid Society Collection

HOW THE ORPHAN TRAINS BEGAN

IMMIGRATION

In 1853 the United States began evaluation of railroad routes to the Pacific, sending mapping announcements to Europe and the rest of the world. Praises went forth, inviting people to come to America and obtain "free land." As a result, the United States received a large number of immigrants. Steamship agents and railroad companies attracted the rest with descriptions of "the land of opportunity." Port cities became overcrowded, with assorted jobs filled by cheap labor. New York City had the largest influx of immigrants. Many made long overland journeys, but countless others stayed in the city. A host of urban ills, including poverty, disease, alcoholism, job competition, and lack of resources led to instability and desperation.

Sometimes families were left with little choice but to abandon their children to the city streets.

THE NEW YORK CHILDREN'S AID SOCIETY

The Children's Aid Society was under the auspices of the Brace Farm School, the Industrial Schools, and Newsboys Lodging Homes. Charles Loring Brace and friends founded the Children's Aid Society in 1853–54. Brace saw orphaned, half-orphaned, and runaway children become waifs of the city. Envisioning new lives for these destitute youngsters, Brace devised a plan to send them away from overpopulated city streets to find family homes in the West. He believed the West had "many spare places at the table of life" and a wholesome atmosphere in which to raise children. This excellent plan was not totally satisfactory for all children. Some went to good homes, but others were instead mistreated.

Upon arrival, children were grouped upon stages, on station platforms, in town halls, or on wooden boxes, and prospective parents were asked to choose a child by personal viewing. Thus the phrase put up for adoption became known. Boys may have had their muscles examined as potential farm laborers. Similarly, teeth, stature, and visible medical issues were considered.

THE NEW YORK FOUNDLING HOSPITAL

In 1869 Sister Mary Irene Fitzgibbons and the Sisters of Charity founded the New York Foundling Hospital. Crime seemed to follow poverty, and the most monstrous crime of all was infanticide. The Sisters were child savers, too, but reserved safekeeping to infants and young children. The Foundling Hospital's children usually aged between one and six years, though some were preteen, rode on trains affectionately called "baby trains," "mercy trains," or "baby specials." This organization sent nearly as many children west as did the Children's Aid Society. The New York Foundling Hospital and the Children's Aid Society were two of the largest East Coast agencies placing children in the West.

INDENTURED APPLICATION

The New York Foundling Hospital commissioned prospective parents to apply for a child in advance. Clergy and city officials announced the need for family homes to local parishes and citizens. Prospective parents could specify the age, gender, and hair and eye color they sought in a child. The New York Foundling Hospital carried an indenture system formulating a contract requiring parents needed to clothe, educate, and provide financially for the child until the age of eighteen. The form essentially guaranteed room and board in exchange for labor. A child could be sent back to New York if placement proved unsatisfactory. The expectation was that the contract could be dismissed in favor of adoption.

SEVENTY FIVE YEARS OF ORPHAN TRAINS

Between 1854 and 1929 over 250,000 children from the urban East Coast, predominantly New York, were placed on what became known as "the orphan trains." This one-way trip was designed to relocate homeless, neglected, and abandoned children to points west across America. It was the largest mass migration of children to take place in American history.

The New York Foundling Hospital on Sixty-eighth and Lexington Street.

The New York Foundling Hospital Collection

THE CHILDREN'S AID SOCIETY OF NEW YORK

Charles Loring Brace

The Children's Aid Society Collection

Charles Loring Brace was born in Litchfield, Connecticut, on June 19, 1826, later in life becoming an educated ordained Methodist minister and changing direction to become a social worker. In 1852, at age twenty six as Brace ministered to the poor of Blackwell's Island (now known as Roosevelt's Island) and to the poor at the Five Points Mission, he decided he wanted to fulfill his humanitarian efforts in the streets rather than in the churches. He was aware of the impoverished lives of children in New York City, and he concentrated on improving their futures. A year later, in 1853, he established the Children's Aid Society.

Brace witnessed many children living their lives in poverty, their parents abusing alcohol, engaging in criminal activity, and seemingly unfit. He detected children whose dedicated parents were too poor to care for their off- spring. He observed children begging for money, selling newspapers or matches on street corners, and stealing for survival.

These children became known as "street Arabs," "waifs of the city," or "the dangerous classes." The area around Tenth Avenue, referred to as Misery Row, was the hotbed for crime and poverty, where orphans and runaways found themselves drifting into destitution. The old shed of Eighteenth and Nineteenth Streets was worse. Such was the severity of child poverty in 1854 that the estimated number of homeless children in New York City soared to 34,000.

Brace focused on finding jobs and training for the destitute children so that they could help themselves. His efforts brought forth social reforms, including free kindergartens and dental clinics, job placements, training programs, reading rooms, and lodging houses for the newsboys.

Brace served as executive secretary and supervisor of the foster care program for thirty-seven years. He died in 1890 from Bight's disease. Subsequently, Brace's sons and others took over duties of the Children's Aid Society. Brace's emigration plan (now known as the orphan trains) sending children west to new family homes throughout the United States, continued until 1929, when transfers ended due to legislative law.

Children Want HOMES

THE CHILDREN'S AID SOCIETY OF NEW YORK

The orphan trains transported the children who were removed from lodge houses, orphanages, private homes, and the city streets of New York and other East Coast locations to settlements where local organizers created interest in the children. Circulars were placed throughout the towns. Newspaper advertisements notified locals of the date and time of the children's arrival as well as naming a viewing location.

Once the train arrived in a town, boys and girls were brought to opera houses, schools, or local town halls to be placed on stages or platforms. Community members and prospective parents could meet and choose a child. Brace did away with the indenture system so the child could leave a home if placement proved unsatisfactory. By 1920 the Children's Aid Society placed nearly 150,000 children.

Indeterminate numbers of placements from the New York Foundling Hospital and other East Coast orphanages combined to become the largest mass migration and resettlement of children in American history.

Homes Wanted For Children

A Company of Orphan Children

of different ages in charge of an agent will arrive at your town on date herein mentioned. The object of the coming of these children is to find homes in your midst, especially among farmers, where they may enjoy a happy and wholesome family life, where kind care, good example and moral training will fit them for a life of self-support and usefulness. They come under the auspices of the New York Children's Aid Society. They have been tested and found to be well-meaning boys and girls anxious for homes.

The conditions are that these children shall be properly clothed, treated as members of the family, given proper school advantages and remain in the family until they are eighteen years of age. At the expiration of the time specified it is hoped that arrangements can be made whereby they may be able to remain in the family indefinitely. The Society retains the right to remove a child at any time for just cause, and agrees to remove any found unsatisfactory after being notified. Remember the time and place. All are invited. Come out and hear the address. Applications may be made to any one of the following well-known citizens, who have agreed to act as a local committee to aid the agent in securing homes.

A.J. Hammond, H.W. Parker, Geo. Baxter, J.F. Damon, J.P. Humes, H.N. Welch, J.A. Armstrong, F.L. Durgin.

This distribution of Children is by Consent of the State Board of Control, and will take place at the

G.A.R. Hall, Winnebago, Minn.
Friday, Jan. 11, 1907, at 10:30 a.m. @ 2 p.m.

H.D. Clarke, State Agent   Office: 105 East 22nd St.
Dodge Center, Minn.   New York City

ORPHAN TRAIN AGENTS OF THE NEW YORK CHILDREN'S AID SOCIETY AND THE NEW YORK FOUNDLING HOSPITAL

A few belongings went with the children transported by streetcar to New York's Grand Central Railway Station. Arrangements were made with train companies for transportation, and a minimum of two agents traveled with the children along the train routes.

Enough food stretched for one day, and while the agent in charge telegraphed ahead to train stations along the way for fresh supplies. Companies of children generally switched trains in Chicago or St. Louis before continuing their journey to destinations extending west of the divide.

AGENTS: THE CHILDREN'S AID SOCIETY AGENTS

Miss C.M. Anderson, Miss H. Baxter, Alice A. Bogardus, Mary Bogardus, C.L. Brace, James P. Brace, Robert N. Brace, Mr. Bugbee, Mr. G. Calder, H.D. Clarke, Clarabelle Comstock, Mr. Dupey, Mrs. M.M. Elston, H. Friedgens, Charles Fry, Georgia Greenleaf, Rudolph Heig, Anna Laura Hill, P.C. Hill, Mr. L.W. Holste, H.A. Holt, Miss Jewell, Nora P. Johnson, Frederick K. King, Miss S.S. Lancaster, W.J. McCully, Mr. J. Mathews, Mr. J.C. Morgan, R.L. Neill, Charles O'Connor, E.H. Opitz, Mr. William Church

Osburn, Mrs. Peterson, Emile Reck, Mr. Roberts, A. Schlegel, J.W. Shields, Miss Sinclaire, E.P. Smith, Hattie McKim Swan, J.W. Swan, Mr. B.W. Tice, Mr. C.C. Tracy, Mr. E.E. Trott, Mr. F. Delano Weekes, Everett Jansen Wendel, Dr. Geo. G. Wheelock, and E. Wright.

THE NEW YORK FOUNDLING HOSPITAL AGENTS

Joseph C. Butler, Robert Curran, Miss Grace Holburton, Florence A. Murray, Charles P. O'Hara, Mr. Joseph O'Shea, Anna Spallen, Mr. Splane, Geo. Whiting Swayne, and M.H. Underhill.

Nurses and Sisters of Charity accompanied and cared for the children throughout the entire journey. The Foundling Hospital commissioned the clergy in town parishes to act as a screening committee for prospective parents and child.

BELOW:
Agents Anna Laura Hill and B.W. Tice with a company of new arrivals in 1909, Lebanon, Missouri.

The Children's Aid Society Collection

H.D. Clarke.
The Children's Aid Society Collection

Plainfield Township, New York, native H.D. Clarke became interested in the Children's Aid Society's emigration plan. While living in Dodge Center, Minnesota, Clarke became a full-time placing and visiting agent for the society, traveling thousands of miles each year caring for the children.

THE NEW YORK FOUNDLING HOSPITAL

The New York Times
August 15, 1896
Credit: The New York Times page 3

SISTER M. IRENE

Foundress of the New York Foundling Hospital
Born May 11, 1823. Died August 14, 1896.

Sister Mary Irene Has Died

Sister Mary Irene, who for twenty-seven years was at the head of the work of saving the lives of homeless infants in New York City, has died. The malady from which she had suffered patiently for forty years, and which ended her life at 7:30 a.m. yesterday morning was heart disease, but the primary cause of her death was the heat.

Her secular name was Mary Irene Fitzgibbon, born in Kensington, England, May 11, 1823. Her parents came to New York when she was nine years old. After education in a parish school, she was determined to become a Sister of Charity. She was received into the community of that sisterhood at Mount St. Vincent on January 15, 1850, and was sent as a novice to St. Peter's School in Barclay Street, although the school of St. Peter's Church was under the charge of the Sisters of Charity. Her executive ability and skill led to her speedy advancement, and in five years from her entrance into St. Peter's School as a novice, she was appointed supervisor.

History of the New York Foundling Hospital

First home of the New York
Foundling Hospital at
17 East Twelfth Street 1869-70.

The New York Foundling Hospital Collection

There were no provisions made by the City of New York for the care of abandoned children until the late 1860s. Waifs picked up by policemen were taken to Blackwell's Island and cared for by aged paupers. Few of the young survived infancy.

The need of an asylum for foundlings similar to those in Europe was supported by many charitable people, and was often considered by the Sisters of Charity, into whose care fell many waifs left by night at the doors of mission houses or on the steps of churches.

Archbishop (later Cardinal) McCloskey urged Mother Mary Jerome, the Mother Superior of the Sisters of Charity to undertake the work of providing for the foundlings. He appointed Sister Mary Irene and two others in 1869 to establish a home for foundlings.

Sister Mary Irene studied the workings of the asylums for infants in operation in Baltimore and Washington, and then she looked for an opportunity to start a similar one in New York.

Sister Mary Irene's only capital was a five-dollar bill given to her by Mother Jerome, and so she sought aid among charitable women and soon formed a society with Paul Thebaund as president and Mrs. Terence Donnelly, Mrs. Eugene Kelly, Mrs. John Fox, Mrs. T.J. Daly, Mrs. A. Jaffrey, and Mrs. G. Schermerhorn serving as officers. Enough money was raised to rent and furnish a small house at 17 East Twelfth Street, where the New York Foundling Hospital opened on October 11, 1869. The building was situated on the north side of the street between Fifth Avenue and University Place, and within a month forty-five children were admitted to the institution.

Foundling hospitals had been established in nearly all the large cities of Europe, the earliest in Milan in 787. Montpellier, Rome, Hanover, Paris, and Venice quickly set up similar institutions. In France alone there were 141 such hospitals, in Holland two, and in Belgium seventeen. A large number were founded in Russia; one was built on a twenty-eight-acre grounds.

Money was needed to carry on the Sisters' work, and to provide it, Samuel S. Cox delivered a lecture that brought $10,000 to the hospital. Dennis O'Donoghue proffered a subscription ball to bring in another $6,500, and private gifts were given by Louis White ($10,000), Mrs. Ceballos ($5,000), and Mr. Higgins ($5,000). Other monetary donations ranged from $1,000 to $4,000.

Within a year, the hospital was moved to a larger building on Washington Square overlooking the park. Within another year, this building became inadequate, and plans were drawn up in 1872 for the construction of an innovative group of buildings.

Second home of the New York Foundling Hospital at 3 North Washington Square 1870-73.

The New York Foundling Hospital Collection

The New York City police often found abandoned babies in the streets, ash barrels, and other out-of-the-way places.

THE NEW YORK FOUNDLING HOSPITAL

In 1870 the legislature passed an act empowering the city to grant the asylum (the name asylum was attached to any place that cared for orphans or other persons requiring specialized care; later the name changed to hospital as the facility became a multi-functional organization employing on-staff physicians and nurses to care for the children) an appropriation of $100,000 for a building, on the condition that an equal amount be raised from private sources. A committee of men was formed to raise the sum by organizing a fair in November 1871. For weeks before the date a wagon rolled slowly through the streets of New York, day after day, carrying a tolling bell to remind the people of the needs of the home for foundlings. The fair yielded $71,500. The entire block between Third and Lexington Avenues and Sixty-eighth and Sixty-ninth Streets was secured, and a hospital building was erected.

Credit: The New York Foundling Hospital Collection

NEW YORK FOUNDLING HOSPITAL

| Maternity Hospital | West Wing | Administrative Building | East Wing | Children's Hospital |

——1880—— |————1873————| ——1882——

Third home of the NYFH at 175 East 68th Street.

19

For years a cradle stood outside the New York Foundling Hospital doors, into which infants were deposited, chiefly by night. Any mother could leave a child she could no longer care for, with no questions asked. The arrivals were numerous that the Sisters decided to surround the reception of infants with some formality, and the cradle was taken into the vestibule, where mothers who desired to abandon their offspring were obliged to speak with the Sisters before leaving.

Initially mothers were not received into the hospital, but not long after the new hospital opened, the policies changed. A young woman once came with her baby and pleaded with the Sisters to let her stay with her child. As provisions had been made for foundlings only, she was refused, but a few hours later she reappeared begging to be allowed to remain. She offered to work for the Sisters and nurse another child as well as her own. This proposal decided both her fate and the hospital's future policy.

Soon infants were "boarded out" for nursing to mothers who had recently lost their baby or to those with a newborn. The wet nurse received ten dollars a month to care for each little charge. She was required to regularly present the children at the hospital for inspection. Nursing mothers were visited at frequent intervals to see how they were treating their foster children. This approach saved many infant's lives and alleviated hospital quarters filled to excess. In 1880 a Maternity Hospital was added to the structure, and later an administrative building and a Children's Hospital were located at the Third Avenue end of the property.

The number of children in the hands of the Sisters became so great that a means of easing the responsibility had to be found. Directly, an agent from the hospital was sent out to several districts across the United States to find homes for the children, who ranged in age from one to four years old. Before long, thousands would be adopted by rural families. The first placement was arranged in the state of Maryland; children would eventually travel farther west.

The hospital had given shelter to tens of thousands of foundlings and provided assistance to countless mothers. From its inception until 1959, records indicate the Foundling Hospital cared for 107,286 infants.

Thousands of infants laid their head upon the pillow of this historical cradle, where mothers abandoned their off-spring.

The New York Foundling Hospital Collection

The New York Times
May 24, 1917
Credit: The New York Times page 12

Sister Teresa Vincent; Foundlings Guardian Dies

Sister Teresa Vincent, Mother Superior of the New York Foundling Asylum, 175 East Sixty-eighth Street, died there yesterday morning after a brief illness. She had been in the sisterhood for fifty-seven years and was one of the co-founders of the asylum forty-eight years ago. For the last twenty-eight years she was the person in charge.

Between 2,700 and 5,000 foundlings were cared for yearly under her direction, and success was in great measure due to her efforts. Her personal influence was applied to aiding unfortunate women.

Before she took the veil her name was Miss Jane Mc Crystal, born July 24, 1842. St. Patrick's Cathedral will hold a solemn Mass Saturday at 10:30 a.m.

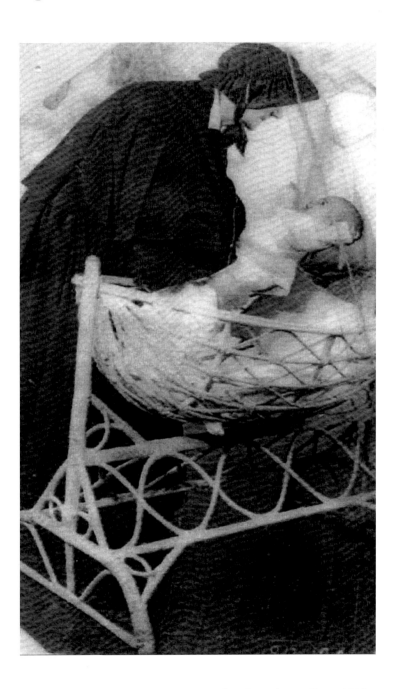

Sister Teresa Vincent accepting an infant from the cradle in 1917.

The New York Foundling Hospital Collection

The New York Foundling Hospital Collection

Sample of indenture form cover

Members of the clergy in towns along the railroad routes were notified that the Foundling Hospital had children in need of homes. Announcements were made to congregation members, asking for volunteers to take the children. Prospective parents could apply for a child in advance and state preferences regarding age, gender, and hair and eye color. The Sisters selected the requested children, believing if a family got a child that "fit in," everyone would be better served.

The New York Foundling Hospital used an indenture system when placing children with new families. The form described various policy terms and gave the Foundling Home legal recourse without court involvement should a placement prove unsatisfactory.

Indentured children who were not legally adopted were ineligible to become heir to a family's estate, unless a will was in place indicating the indentured child was to receive an inheritance.

The New York Times
May 20, 1900
Credit: The New York Times page 21

Hospital Babies Tagged - Avoiding Confusion

At the New York Foundling Asylum the babies are marked with little cards tied to the waists of their little gowns. Two babies sleep together in a crib, and when the children are undressed for the night the cards stay with the clothing worn by the child ready to be put on in the morning. When a baby is sent out to board (infants were often boarded-out for wet-nursing) or wherever the child goes, the card is worn marked with all necessary information and assigned hospital number. These numbers date from the first child received, and include all of the children either born at the hospital or those taken in. There are 31,000 children to date.

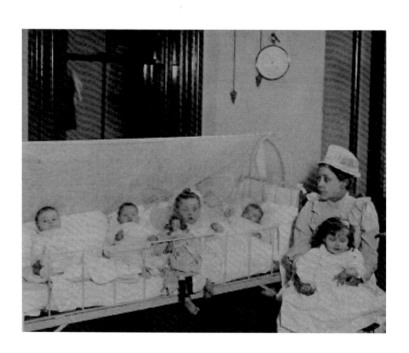

Tagged babies amid a netted crib.

The New York Foundling Hospital Collection.

The New York Foundling Hospital

Sisters of Charity
No. 175 East 68th Street
New York City

THE NOTICE OF ARRIVAL

No. (assigned Foundling Hospital number)

Child's Name
Any Town USA
Any State USA

We take pleasure in notifying you that the little (boy/girl) which you so kindly ordered will arrive at (any town), on the (train name) train on (day, month, and year) on the train due to arrive at (time, a.m. p.m.), and ask that you kindly be at the Railway Station to receive child 30 minutes before the train is due, and avoid any possibility of missing connection, as the train will not wait should you not be there.

The name of the child, date of birth, and name and address of party to whom child is assigned will be found sewn in the coat or collar of the boy, and in the hem of the dress of the girl.

This receipt must be signed in ink by both husband and wife, and is to be given up in exchange for the child who will have a corresponding number.

Yours very truly,
Sisters of Charity

THE RECEIPT OF CHILD

We beg to acknowledge receipt of the little orphan as numbered above and promise faithfully to raise said child in the Roman Catholic faith and to send (him, her) to school and give (him, her) all the advantages that we would give to a child of our own, and report to the Sisters of Charity as to health and general condition when requested, notifying them of any change in address.

Signature of Husband _____

Signature of Wife_____

Street Address _____

_____

Date_____Town_____State _____

The fourth home of the New York Foundling Hospital (1958-88) at 1175 Third Avenue. No child placed on an orphan train from this establishment as the trains stopped transport of the precious cargo in 1929. In September 1988, the Foundling Hospital relocated to its fifth and present home at 590 Avenue of the Americas, New York City.

FORSAKEN

Your tiny hand grips my finger
Our eyes meet one last time,
Charming features etched forever
All I see is you.

The moments pass quickly
I know it's almost time,
I hold you close afraid to let you go
Reluctantly, I hand you over.

Tears fall like rain
Matching an unparallel rhythm,
I stare into another time and place
Will I ever be complete again?

My heart aches
Yet you will never leave me,
For in my mind
You'll belong to me forever!

© 2008 Renée Wendinger

Letters Left by Mothers

Five leather-bound albums entitled "Letters Left on Babies by Their Mothers" surround a stack of papers once placed in an area at the New York Foundling Hospital's headquarters at Avenue of the Americas and Sixteenth Street. Snippets of unique sentiment remain fixed within the folds of the letters, a piece of fabric torn from a dress or a ribbon from Ulysses S. Grant's re-election campaign. These are responsive trinkets that would one day identify children so that their mothers might claim them.

A good deal has changed since these letters arrived at the Foundling Hospital. Orphanages have been replaced with foster care; unmarried mothers are not so aggressively scrutinized; clergy and police officers no longer decide the destinies of children. These letters reveal more than the adversity of surrendering a child for adoption; rather, they provide evidence that foundlings have always been born more of poverty than of neglect.

Samplings of letters are taken from these collections.

LETTERS LEFT BY MOTHERS

Brooklyn
Nov. 23, 1869

Dear Sister,

I now sit down to write to you a few lines but I hardly know what to say, for when I inform you that I am the mother of the child left on Thanksgiving night between the hours of 8 and 9 o'clock without even a slip of paper to tell you the name of the child left in your care, my heart aches so much, but I knew that I was leaving her in good hands.

Although I have been unfortunate, I am neither low nor degraded, and am in hopes of one day claiming my child. Her name is Jone...born on 5 of October 1869 between the hours of 3 and 4 o'clock in the morning...she had a piece of canton flannel with a little blue and white cloud tied around her head and little red and white socks on her feet. If the prayers of an unfortunate creature like myself will do any good, offered to the mercy of God in heaven...for you know that every night on bended knees I pray for you. I am very sorry that I, having nothing to send you this time, am in hope there will be a day when I shall be able to pay you for all your trouble.

Unsigned

Most Holy Redeemer Church
Sister M. Irene, Superioress
Dec. 10, 1869

Respected Sister,

Would you oblige our Reverend Father Rector Leimgruber in taking this poor child into the Asylum? He has been happily saved from being murdered this morning by his unfortunate mother. She told me that she gives up all claims on him. I gave private baptism to the child.

Respectfully yours,
Francis Eberhardt, C.S.S.R.

1869

These two dollars is to have this child christened Willie. Do not be afraid of the sores on his face; it is nothing but ringworm. You will remember this badge. Included with this letter is a colorful cloth badge that reads, "General Grant our next President."

Unsigned

July 1870

To the Sisters of the House,

Necessity compels me to part with my darling boy. I leave him, hoping and trusting that you will take good care of him. Will you let some good nurse take charge of him and will you try to find some kind hearted lady to adopt him and love him as her own while he is young that he may know that she is his one mother? It would break my heart to have him grow up without a mother to love, and care for him. God only knows the bitter anguish of my heart in parting with the little dear; still if it costs me my life, I am obliged to give him up.

He is just from the breast, he has been sick with his bowels, they have not been right for a long time. I have cried and worried over him so much that I think my milk hurt him. I think a change of milk with good care will make him well soon. I got these things, thinking I could keep him, but as I can not they may be of use to you. I shall always take an interest in this Institution.

He is 4 weeks old. Will you please remember his given name, and if he is adopted, request that they will not change his name; so at some future day, if that name should be asked for, you will be able to tell what became of him or where he is. Perhaps you will think me very particular, but if any mother will take it home to her own heart, and think how she would feel to have her dear little boy torn from her breast, I think they would excuse me.

This is the last time I can speak of him as mine, and if in years to come I could hear that he had a home and friends, I could die in peace. On the other hand, if I should never hear, it would haunt the day of my death. Please excuse all that you think is not right, but for God's sake remember the last request of a heart broken mother.

Unsigned

The New York Foundling Hospital Collection

Police Department of the
City of New York
Precinct No. 20
Aug. 5, 1872

To the Superior of
the Foundling Hospital,
   We have arrested a woman for intoxication and
vagrancy at 11 this P.M. She has an infant about
3 weeks old, and she wanted to destroy it. So it is
not proper to leave it in her charge, and even of
she was sober, she is not in a fit state to take care
of it.
   The child will not live if it does not have nour-
ishment. If you will take care of it, also the older
one, until tomorrow, I will have them sent to the
Commissioners of the Public Charities.
   We have tried to get some of her people to take
care of this infant. They all refuse. I do not know
what else to do with these children other than
leave them in your kind protection for this night,
and by so doing, very much oblige.

Yours Respectfully,
Charles W. Coffry, Capt.

LETTERS LEFT BY MOTHERS

1875

Dear Sisters,
   By the love of God be so kind as to take this
poor orphan child, and if she should die, please
to bury her for me, and I will be very happy.
You must not think that I have neglected her. I
have worked very hard to pay her board but I
can't afford to bury her.
   So, by the love of God, take this little child in.
May God Bless you all for your kindness to all
the little sufferers. This little child has suffered
since she was born, and I have paid debts but
I have not paid all but I shall. My husband is
dead, and I have nobody to help me. Be kind to
my little lamb. May the great God receive her
into Heaven where she will be loved by God.

Unsigned

May 22, 1873

   This off-spring is the fruit of a brutality on the
person of this poor but decent woman, and to
cover her shame of being too poor to support the
children. There are two from her husband. She
is obliged to resort to this extreme measure. The
child is not yet baptized.

Day old infant left by
Dr. J.J. Brennan

St. Patrick's Cathedral
New York
Aug. 28, 1875

Sister Irene,
   The child in question is indeed an object of
charity. The mother is in danger of death; she
is but 15 years of age, and without means of
providing for the child. The child has been
baptized in this church.

Yours in Christ,
Rev. William Hogan

Dec. 1, 1875

Dear Sister,
  Alone and deserted, I must put my little one with you for a time. I would willingly work and take care of her but no one will have me and her too. All say they would take me if she was 2 or 3 years old, so not knowing what to do with her and not being able to pay her board, I bring her to you knowing you will be as kind to her as to the many others who are under your care, and I will get work and try hard to be able to relieve you of the care when I can take her to work with me. She is only 3 weeks old, and I have not had her christened or anything.
  No one knows how awful it is to separate from their child but a mother, but I trust you will be kind as the only consolation I have if I am spared, and nothing prevents, I will lead an honest life that the father of us all will permit us to be united.

Signed,
A Mother

1875

  For the love of God, and his holy mother, will you keep the little baby who was left in the crib last night; I will give anything you require. Her father is a wicked Orangeman. I told him it was dead because I want to have her raised a Roman Catholic, and have nursed out. I will pay all the expenses.
  Will you, dear Sisters, remember a kind mother's heart? If I do not see her again, I will never do any good on this earth. I work at dress making for a living. My husband gives me but a third of his earnings because I am a Roman Catholic. Write to Father Farrell, Barclay Street Church, state circumstances to him. Pray to the Blessed Virgin for me to help me through.

Unsigned

LETTERS LEFT BY MOTHERS

November 1876

Miss Brock,
  You can keep the baby or you can put it in the street or not, for I will not pay for it, for it has no father nor anyone to look after it. So you better put it away for I will not pay for it. Child's name: Alpheus.

– left by Father Reilly

St. Patrick's Church Rectory
263 Mulberry Street
July 15, 1884

Dear Sister,
  I have an unfortunate girl in my parish that has given birth to an illegitimate child. She is so circumstanced that if it were known it would greatly injure her, and at the same time gives rise to a great deal of scandal among her friends. She is truly repentant, and has brought the child to me to be baptized. (His name is Louis.) I therefore request of you the favor to receive the child in the asylum, and free her from the burden which she has been so unfortunate to bring upon herself. Greatly oblige.

Yours respectfully,
Rev. L.A. Mazziatta

ORPHANS
IN THE NEWS

ORPHANS IN THE NEWS:

The Children's Aid Society

St. Cloud (Minnesota) Times
July 16, 1873

Credit: The Minnesota Historical Society

Homes for the Homeless

On last Saturday Mr. Charles R. Fry, an agent for the Children's Aid Society of New York, arrived in this city with eighteen boys for whom homes were wanted. They were taken to the Presbyterian Church, where a dinner had been provided by the ladies. After this was over with, persons who had made application for a boy made their selection. The greatest care was exercised that only good treatment for the boys could be expected should anyone be allowed to have one of them. The lads were bright, intelligent looking little fellows, and ranged from about six to fourteen years of age. Everybody was surprised to find there were more applications than boys. Mr. Fry says he never met with so kind and hearty a welcome for the homeless ones under his charge than this place.

The following list of those who took the orphans will show that the boys received good homes:

Dr. E. Mariatt; Geo. E. Fuller; F.H. Owen; Charles T. Smith; S.J. Shepard; H.J. Fowler; F.M. Shook; B. Overbeck; and Rev. E.V. Campbell of St. Cloud. Ed. Hall; J.D. Hyke; H. Caywood; Justus Carpenter and A. Smith of Sauk Rapids. F.O. Wiley of Santiago. Charles Neal, D.A. Hoyt and E. Kidder of Maine Prairie.

The Sentinel, Martin County, Minnesota
October 13, 1882
Credit: The Minnesota Historical Society

CHILD	PLACEMENTS: (City or Township)
Andrew Spring age 16	John Watson—Fraser
Geo. O'Donnell age 14	Geo. Tanner—Fairmont
Michele P/Fu-pisek age 15	C.C. Smith—Rolling Green
Edward Naber age 16	Geo. Smith—Fairmont
John J. Travis age 9	Wm. Clark—Fairmont
William Styles age 13	Alonzo B. Hall—Center Creek
William James Hope age 12	Fred Peterson—Fairmont
Henry Styles age 11	J.W. Moore—Fraser
K.J. Sui-ille age 12	R.N. Taylor—Rutland
Alice Boyle age 14	Mrs. Geo. Tanner—Fairmont
Nora Logne age 14	Mrs. John Tanner—Fairmont
Alice Buckley age 15	Mrs. Barnett—Westford
Carrie Douglass age 18	Capt. Weberland—Rolling Green
Henrietta Thompson age 15	R.J. McCadden—Rutland
Samuel Dowling age 18	H.R. Rouse—Fairmont
E. Ehrmann age 18	W.G. McCadden—Rutland
J. O'Brien age 18	Alonzo Hall—Center Creek
J. Lutirell age 18	G.S. Livermore—Fairmont
R. Kempton age 18	R. Boudrye—Fairmont
R. Brown age 13	John Tanner—Fairmont
E. Corbin age 18	A. St. John—Welcome
Nelly Kinny age 13	Byron St. John—Fraser

The Sentinel, Martin County, Minnesota
October 27, 1882
Credit: The Minnesota Historical Society

CHILD	PLACEMENTS: (City or Township)
John Rose age 8	F. Bickel/Rickel—Fairmont
Willie Thompson age 6	R.W. Thomas—Fairmont
Charles Brown age 5	Mrs. Mary Curtis—Rolling Green
Freddie Lester age 4	A.C. Gilbert—Rutland
Robert Reil/Rail age 5	A.R. Johnson—Rutland
Evelyn McGlynn age 5	L.S. Parker—Fairmont
Philip Darens age 7	James Hendry—Fraser
John Briscoe age 5	E.M. Hyatt—Fairmont
Charles E. Smith age 7	Mrs. M.E. St. John—Fraser
Jeremiah Shaw age 4	S.R. Older—Pleasant Prairie
Stephen Firicette age 15	James German—Fraser
Robert Taylor age 11	Alvin Woodbury—Pleasant Prairie
Donald Monroe age 9	R.A. Chambers—Pleasant Prairie
Joseph ?yons age 6	Charles E. Wood—Tenhassen
Henry Shaffer age 6	Ezra Graham—Tenhassen
Willie Snedicker age 6	J.R. Watson—Jay
Mary Forti age 6	Edward Whelpley—Chain Lake Center
William Reasler age ?	O.S. Burdick—Chain Lake Center
Charles Haug/Haag age 18	J.H. Smith—Nashville Center
Joseph Burrows age 18	Orrin Bacon—Nashville Center
Geo. Thompkins age 6	Joshua Betts—Nashville Center
Eddie Frost age ?	Thomas Humphries-Fairmont
Edward Zeeler age 5 or 8	A. St. John—Welcome
Henry Straiton age 16	J.M. Hasse—Fountanelle
Daniel Maby age 4	Tom Allen—Center Creek

Rochester (Minnesota) Post
Eyota, Minnesota
February 8, 1888
Credit: The Minnesota Historical Society

A company of homeless boys from the Children's Aid Society of New York are expected at this place on the 17th instant. The boys are in charge of the Society's agent Mr. A. P. Stockwell, and will be aided in finding them suitable homes by a committee of our leading citizens. We understand some of the farmers in this vicinity have already decided to furnish some of these unfortunate boys' homes.

———— ⁓w⁓ ————

Minneapolis (Minnesota) Journal
January 13, 1899
Credit: The Minnesota Historical Society

CHILDREN FIND HOMES
Company of Homeless Children from New York Placed with Families Here

Thirteen homeless children from New York City, ten boys and three girls, were found homes with families in the vicinity yesterday. The children arrived on the 9:16 passenger, and came direct from New York City in charge of Mr. E. Trott, a representative of the New York Children's Aid Society who will remain for a day or two visiting the homes in which they have been placed and see that all are agreeably located.

The children were all well clothed and had the appearance of being bright and well behaved. It was an affecting scene at the hall where they were taken for distribution. Saddened by the thought of being separated from one another, the children burst into tears, and more than one of the people gathered there, touched with sympathy and pity for the little ones, slyly wiped a tear away. Specially affecting were the acts of the little brother and sister who embraced and cried over one another. The placement of the children was quickly arranged for, and in a few hours they separated going into strange homes among strange people. Below are the given names of the children, and the name of the persons in whose homes they were placed:

Geo. Smith age 11 to Geo. Letherman
William Stevenson age 12 to F. Hoffman Jr.
Fred Clark age 13 to F.S. Reynolds
James A. Hamilton age 14 to G.C. Bice
James May age 10 to Fred Bremer
Edward May age 13 to Lewis Gardne

Amelia Engle age 9 to C.G. Newell
Pearl Galdo age 3 to I.E. Ondler
Geo. Galdo age 5 to Geo. Oldridge
Harry Johnson age 11 to Joshua Winn
James Mayne age 8 to E.R. Watson
Anton Jnouskey age 13 and his half sister Tilla Remer departing for Lime Springs, Iowa

Paris, Arkansas 1909

Credit: The Children's Aid Society and the Orphan Train Complex Collection

Homes Secured For
Orphan Children in Paris, Arkansas

CHILD	PLACED	CHILD	PLACED
Margaret Phelan age 9	Louis Girard	Edward Beatty age 8	J.P Rider
Louise Van Epps age 9	Miss Eva Corley	Joe Martin age 8	Joe Willman
Una Tielinen age 11	J.E. Alvis	Sarah Phelan age 7	Geo. M. Zeller
Irvin Van Epps age 11	Walter Butler	Frank Pauquette age 2	J.J. Swain
Anna Stephen age 13	Abel Nehus	Harry Proper age 10	A.M. Biggs
Catherine Phelan age 13	Frank Binz Sr.	Marry Smith age 8	G.H. McDaniel
Earl Peck age 13 & Kenneth Peck age 7	Sid Roady	Edward Davis age 7	Don B. Hoopes
Grace Van Epps age 6	J.R. Plunkett	Willie Pauquette age 4	John Parke

———————— ⚬⚬⚬ ————————

Paris, Arkansas 1917

Homes Wanted for Homeless Children

The Children's Aid Society of New York on Friday November 2, 1917, transported to Paris a company of homeless children, both Protestant and Catholic for the purpose of finding them homes.

These children come from different orphanages and institutions, some of them in your own state, and have been well trained and selected with care to fit the new home life which they are about to enter and if any mistake be made in the choice of a child, or for any reason the child is not satisfactory, the Society will remove the child and bear the expense and trouble for return.

If you apply for a child you should be prepared to satisfy the Society that you will furnish the comforts of a home, that you will treat the little one as a real member of your family by taking the place of father and mother as nearly as possible; that you will give the child the education and moral training to become a respectable and self-supporting citizen.

If you have never had a child in your home, you know but little of a home in its fullest sense, such as nature and providence intended. It is a great responsibility, it is true, to raise a child properly, but greater pleasure, and the love and labor you bestow on them while small will likely be repaid you many times in later life when you need some one to lean upon, and you will have the satisfaction of knowing that you have done your part of the world's great work.

The children can be seen on the above date at the Court House at 2 p.m. We would be glad to have you come and see the children and hear the address.

The following well known citizens have been selected as a committee to assist us in placing these children: W.H. Bennett, M.D.; Rev. Geo. McGlumphy; W.C. Roady cashier of the German-American Bank & Trust Co.; Geo. M. Zeller; W.R. Cherry cashier at the bank of Paris; W.B. Rhyne attorney at law.

You can make an application to any one of them, and you will need their endorsement. Hoping that you will come and aid us, and that you will interest others so that we may find good homes for these dear little ones among you.

P.C. Morgan, Agent—
Wheeler, Arkansas

The New York Times
June 20, 1897

Credit: The New York Times page 12. Sending Foundlings West

SENDING FOUNDLINGS WEST
Mother Superior of the New York Asylum
Defends Robert Curran and Tells of the Practice

CHICAGO— Two Sisters of Charity connected with the New York Foundling, 175 East Sixty-Eighth Street, returned from Chicago yesterday. Robert Curran, the outdoor agent of the asylum, against whom charges have been made that he has been carrying a traffic in little children, selling them at six dollars, is said to be still in that city.

The Mother Superior in charge of the asylum made a statement yesterday in regard to the affair in recommendation and approval of Curran. "Mr. Curran has been our agent for the past twelve years," she said, "and we have implicit confidence in him. He is kind hearted, tender, and a considerate man, and we have innumerable letters from those who have adopted our children testifying to his good character.

"In the case of little Mary, or May Bliss, I find from our records that she had been indentured to Mrs. Lizzie Murphy, in Chicago, but it developed that this woman was not able to provide for the child, and returned her to our agent. A little while afterward, May was indentured to Mrs. Casey, who has become deeply attached to the little girl, and has proved a true mother to her. Mrs. Murphy, I imagine, took the course reported through malice. I can account for her action in no other way.

"No child is indentured or given for adoption until we are satisfied that a good home will be provided. In rare cases, like this one, it happens that those who obtain a child are unable to continue the proper care and so report to us. The child is then taken back and placed elsewhere. We pay all the expenses of the children sent to the West, and accept no money for them, except in cases where the adoption has been arranged in advance.

"Mr. Curran went west two months ago with forty-eight children. He was accompanied by two nurses and two Sisters from the asylum. The two Sisters returned today, and have given the most satisfactory account of the children, not only the ones they accompanied, but many of the others previously sent West by us. They were emphatic in their praises of Mr. Curran. We place 250 to 300 children a year through him, and we have never yet had a complaint against him."

The New York Times
July 10, 1897

Credit: The New York Times page 2

NEW YORK ORPHANS GO WEST
Party of Forty-One Reach Chicago

CHICAGO—- Forty-one children from a New York Foundling Asylum came West today to grow up in the country. Their guardians thought South Bend, Indiana would be a good place for a half dozen of them to take root and flourish. Six were dropped off there as the train passed through the town.

At 3 o'clock thirty-five children on a special car arrived at the Van Buren Street Station in charge of Robert Curran, the agent of the asylum. The children ranged in age from two years to four years. Several people, who came to meet the train to get children, followed the parade closely, and a crowd of passengers joined the throng.

Two of the children went to Chicago families. At 9 o'clock all the rest were starting for their future homes in Michigan. Ten are going to Red Jacket, five to Hancock, six to Marquette, three to Escanaba, six to Bark River, and three to Negaunee. This is the fourth batch of youngsters which has been sent here this year by the New York Asylum.

St. Cloud (Minnesota) Times
June 17, 1899

Credit: The Minnesota Historical Society

GOING TO HOMES

Half a Hundred Orphans Among the Great Northern Passengers Today

An extra coach attached to the Great Northern west bound passenger train this morning was graced by fifty-one children from the Catholic Orphan Asylum of New York City. They ranged in ages from four to six years. The car was in charge of three Sisters of Charity and the children were looked after by a matron. Homes are awaiting each one of the children in Northern Minnesota and North Dakota. They have all been told that they are going on a trip to find papa and momma, and if you ask them where they are going they will tell you so. Each one of the little ones is anxious to see their papa and momma, and every visitor meets with the severest scrutiny from them.

St. Cloud (Minnesota) Times
September 14, 1899

Credit: The Minnesota Historical Society

MANY LITTLE ORPHANS

A Coach Load of New York Orphans Finding Good Homes in Stearns County

A coach containing forty-seven homeless boys and girls were a part of the regular west bound local passenger train on the Great Northern today. Their sweet little faces were glued against the windows as they gazed into strange faces, for the tots were miles and miles distant from the place of their nativity.

They are a second assignment of orphan children from a New York Catholic Foundling Home for whom good homes have been secured in Stearns County.

A gentleman and his wife from New York spent several weeks in the county during the summer and engaged houses for them and now the delivery is being made. The party was in charge of the gentleman and his wife and three or four Sisters of Charity. The little people were spotlessly clean and inviting. Three were received by their future foster parents at the depot here and the others will be distributed at various points along the line in this county.

Special to The New York Times
St. Louis, MO. May 15, 1901
Credit: The New York Times page 2. Foundlings Find Homes

FOUNDLINGS FIND HOMES
Children From a Catholic Asylum Taken to the West
No Redheaded Ones Among Them

By 1910, forty-seven states, Canada, the District of Columbia and the Indian Territory had taken children from the orphan trains under the care of the New York Children's Aid Society, 1854-1929.

The Orphan Train Complex Collection

Fifty-two black, brown, yellow, and flaxen haired children from a New York Roman Catholic Foundling and Orphan Asylum filled a special car at the Union Station this morning, waiting to be adopted.

No red-headed children or children with freckles were among them. Red-headed children, especially those with freckles, are not easily placed in homes, even if their hair is of Titian and the freckles beauty spots.

G. Whiting Swayne, the traveling agent whose duty it is to find homes for about 100 children each year, said today that he had inquired all over the United States into the reason for this, and had invariably been told that red-headed children fought too much, and had bad tempers generally. He does not agree with this verdict, but finds it difficult to defeat a tradition that has stood for many generations.

The children sent to Missouri this year were at the Union Station only a few minutes before they were on their way to their future homes. Thirty departed at 7:35 a.m. in charge of the two Sisters of Charity for farms in Osage County. While five others

started at 8:45 a.m. in the care of Mr. Swayne for homes on farms around Vienna and Viosmann, in Marion County. Fifteen were delivered to their adopted parents at Union Station, five being taken by farmers near Collinsville, Illinois and others by St. Louis farmers.

The children were told that they had been at school and were returning to their parents, a fiction which their adopted parents will continue. The distribution at the Union Station was systematic. Each adopted parent presented a ticket forwarded from New York, with a number corresponding to that on the child assigned to the holder of the ticket. Care was taken to adhere to the preference expressed by the applicant relative to color of hair, sex, and disposition. The distribution attracted considerable attention. In most cases the little ones greeted their new parents as if they recognized them, and were returning after a brief absence.

In finding homes for the

foundlings, Mr. Swayne travels all over the U.S. selecting Roman Catholic families who desire to adopt children. Farmers are chosen exclusively, the theory being that the children are exposed to less temptation on farms than in cities and towns. The arrangements are so perfect that, while the prospective parents do not see the children until they reach them, a small number express dissatisfaction at selections made for them.

"The predominating preference," said Mr. Swayne "is for children with blue eyes and blonde curly hair. The only request ever made for one with red hair that I know of was from a farmer in Indiana. He and his wife had red hair, and they had three little girls with red hair. They wanted a boy with red hair too. It is much easier to place the girls than the boys. Girls are company for a woman on the farm where it sometimes is pretty lonesome."

Special to the Washington Post
Minneapolis, Minnesota
August 22, 1905

Credit: The Minnesota Historical Society

FEARS FOR ORPHANS' FATE
North Dakota Officials Thinks Them Doomed to Drudgery

Last Saturday a special car filled with children, none more than four years old, passed through Minneapolis. Eleven of the little ones, who were sent out by a Foundling Society in New York, were placed in homes near the Twin Cities, and forty in charge of Miss Grace Holburton, of New York, and four men, were sent on to North Dakota. Today

Superintendent Hall of the North Dakota Children's Home at Fargo said that these and other children sent out from the Eastern cities were doomed to drudgery which would amount to serfdom.

Twenty-seven applicants for the orphans, he said, were Russians. Many of them had children of their own, lived on farms far from towns and schools, and

were illiterate and sully. Among these people, who hold aloof from Americans and cling to old Russian customs, in which the orphans would be reared, unless state authorities can prevent it. Expectations are to be handled under an old law which prohibits the importation of needy or orphan children.

The New York Times
May 10, 1906

Credit: The New York Times page 6. Foundlings Sent to Texas

FOUNDLINGS SENT TO TEXAS
Fifty-Eight Children Start for the Homes Procured for Them

Fifty-eight boys and girls from the New York Foundlings and Orphan Asylum at 175 East Sixty-eighth Street started for Texas yesterday, where they are to begin life anew as the adopted children of well to do Texas citizens, who have promised to rear the little ones exactly in the same way that they would their own children. The children started South on the Cromwell steamship Proteus, which will land them at New Orleans. From that city they will proceed to their new homes in the

Lone Star State by the Southern Pacific Railroad.

The entire second cabin of the Proteus was devoted to the youngsters, and judging from their antics before the steamship sailed, they are in for a gay time between this city and New Orleans. Four nurses and one doctor went along to look after the children. Only one child will be adopted into each family. The persons who will adopt the children have all been investigated by the authorities in

charge of the asylum, and it was said on the pier yesterday that there was not a boy or girl in the party that went South that would not be sure of a good home.

Each of the children had a complete outfit of clothing, and toys and picture books plenty to last the voyage. John D. Crimmins was at the pier to see them off. The children ranged in age from eighteen months to five years. There were twenty eight girls and thirty boys.

St. Paul (Minnesota) Pioneer
Thursday October 15, 1908
Credit: The Minnesota Historical Society

A CARLOAD OF BABIES
Sixty-Seven Little Ones Shipped West from New York

A dispatch from Milwaukee says:

There were 67 of them and 67 different varieties. There were babies from two years up to five, all colors, shapes, sizes, and previous conditions of servitude. Little waifs they were, the discard of New York, out in search of a home far from the center of sorrows and woes that they were born into.

On the way to St. Paul from New York a special car with these babies passed through Milwaukee. With the children there were several Sisters of Charity and two trained nurses. The Foundling Hospital of New York is sending them West to deal them out into good homes among the farmers near St. Paul, Minnesota.

When the conductor came out of the car there was a suspicion of moisture in his eyes. "I won't go through there again," he said. "They're happy, and all that, but it's too pitiful. They all wanted to shake hands with me, and caught hold of my hand and looked up at me and smiled as I passed. I suppose they are taught to do it.

There are all kinds, and they are just as sweet as most babies are. It is a shame that they will never know a real mother and father."

The Sisters made the babies beds by placing boards across from seat to seat, for the special car was not a sleeping car. Several babies were piled into one 'bed.' The car accommodated the 67, besides the nurses and Sisters. Long pieces of sheeting were stretched across the tops of the seats to cover the 'beds' to keep out the cinders and dust.

Minneapolis (Minnesota) Journal
October 22, 1909
Credit: The Minnesota Historical Society

CHILDREN ARE WELCOME
Homes for Forty-five Orphans Found in Minnesota Families

Homes have been secured for forty-five orphans that are to be sent to Minnesota from the New York Foundling and Orphans Asylum.

Joseph C. Butler, representing the institution, was in conference today with Rev. T.E. Cullen of the Church of the Immaculate Conception. He said that as soon as he finds Catholic homes for sixty, he will notify the New York Home and the children attended by Sisters and nurses will be sent on. The children are two and three years of age.

Mr. Butler has been in St. Paul for two weeks investigating homes for the children. Most of the offers have come from the country.

Minneapolis/St. Paul, Minnesota
Date unknown

Credit: The Minnesota Historical Society

Orphans
For Adoption

A carload of babies for adoption by Catholic families in the West was sent out last week from an Orphan Asylum conducted by the Sisters of Charity in New York. Forty-five of the sixty-five babies found foster parents in Minnesota. The ease in which suitable places were found for these orphans speaks volumes for the charity of our people. It shows that there are many Catholic families in the state willing to adopt children, and give them all the advantages of a home.

While we have no intention of discouraging those who may be planning to take a child from the Orphans Home, we suggest that, before communicating with those in charge, they assure themselves that they cannot be supplied with one nearer home. In St. Paul and Minneapolis, for example, there are three orphan asylums conducted by Sisters, and in other towns of the state there are diocesan institutions for Catholic children who have been deprived of their natural guardians. Very often it happens that these institutions have boys and girls for whom suitable

St. Paul, Minnesota Union Depot.
Minnesota Historical Society Collection

homes in Catholic families are desired and there is no reason why preference should not be given to them by the Catholics of Minnesota, and of the Northwest. Even if the diocesan orphanages cannot supply the demand made upon them by families anxious to adopt children, it does not necessarily follow that applications must be made to orphanages in the East. Frequently priests and others who are interested in social work know of children for whom suitable homes are desired, and they would be glad to get in touch with people who may wish to adopt a child. If your pastor cannot help you in this matter, why not make an application to the City Missionary of St. Paul or Minneapolis who may be able to help you in this mater. Write to the Rev. L.F. Ryan, 239

The Chicago, Milwaukee and St. Paul Railroad Station, 1901, Minneapolis, Minn. The station was also known as the Milwaukee Road Depot or Station, or directly as the Milwaukee Road.

Minnesota Historical Society Collection

Selby Avenue, St. Paul or to the Rev. M.A. McGrath, 1623 Laurel Avenue, Minneapolis, who will gladly aid you in your laudable and charitable purpose.

Date unknown

Credit: *The New York Foundling Hospital Collection*

The New York Foundling Hospital

If you've ever tried to dress one baby to take on a journey you can imagine something of the flurry there was in the staid and decorous halls of the Foundling Hospital yesterday morning when fifty- six little ones were dressed into caps and hats, mittens and coats, in preparation for the trip.

Nurses bustled frantically about; sweet faced nuns knelt upon the floor smoothing little gowns and pulling up little collars as tenderly as any mother could have done. While the children, too little and too ignorant to understand the significance of what was happening to them, out-wardly sensing a change, lifted up their voices, and wept at being parted from the only home and affection they had ever known.

The oldest of the children was barely four, and the youngest a toddler hardly two and a half. They were just babies, and such adorable babies that it made you want to kidnap every one.

There was Theresa No. 34, with the olive and the rose of far off Italy flaming in her little cheeks. There was Mary, No. 26, dark as a gypsy, with sloe black eyes. There was Helena, No. 31, with melting brown eyes and golden hair. There was Susie, No. 19, with Titian curls above a face of ivory. There was Joseph, No. 30, a regular little brownie. Henry, No. 38, with a tip-tilted nose, and a quizzical little face. There was William, No. 25, a sturdy little lad who had "Bill" written all over him, if any stocky little boy ever did. And so on, through the long list.

They were all prize babies, no matter which one you drew–so intelligent and good looking. It made you believe in the old tradition that fate showers her choicest blessings on the love child to make up for other things it loses. If Santa Claus were a real fairy, he could wave no magic wand nor perform any miracle greater than this.

The New York Foundling Hospital Collection

ORPHANS IN THE NEWS:
The New York Foundling Hospital

New Orleans - 1909

Credit: New Orleans Dominican Sisters Archives

As sixty children disembarked at the train station in New Orleans, Louisiana, Peter J. Frabacher was greeting the train with his nephew John Frey. Frey had asked the Foundling Hospital for a five-year-old boy. As the two men searched the platform for the boy, someone thrust two-year-old Sarah Hunt, No. 59, into Frabacher's arms. Frabacher noticed the tag on the child's dress held the name Sarah. Disappointed, Frey wanted to send the child back to New York, as he had anticipated a boy to inherit his rice plantation one day.

Little Sarah draped her arms around Frabacher's neck, and the restaurant owner decided to take the plunge. Sarah grew up in the Frabacher happy family of fourteen children, and one day she became Sister Mary James of the Dominican Sisterhood in New Orleans. She lived until ninety-nine years of age.

The children arriving at their new states' destination from the New York Foundling Hospital were often too young to remember their train journey west, as the Foundling placed infants through age six. Sarah's white dress, bonnet, and high-top button shoes were typical outfits donned by the one- to three-year-olds. Her ribbon number matched the one her prospective parents held and its color designated her state's final destination.

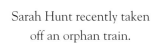

Sarah Hunt recently taken off an orphan train.

The New Orleans Dominican Sisters Collection

The New York Times
March 18, 1910

Credit: The New York Times page 1. The South Calls for Northern Babies

THE SOUTH CALLS FOR NORTHERN BABIES
Foundling Asylum Sent a Carload of Seventy
Last Week and More Are Wanted

—ᴍ—

TEXAS WRITES TO MAYOR
Baptist Clergyman and a Farmer Want One Each-
Asylum's Orphans Sent to New Orleans

To satisfy an unusually active demand for babies, centering chiefly around New Orleans, and southern Louisiana towns, the New York Foundling and Orphans Asylum at Sixty -Eighth Street and Lexington Avenue, sent out a cargo of choice but parentless babies last week in answer to letters from parents in comfortable but childless homes. Since then the quality of the home brighteners sent out has proven to be in such high order, that the institution has been swamped with letters demanding babies, and is now getting ready a second consignment to send Dixie ward in a few weeks.

The last shipment of choice baby freight was sent out in charge of two Sisters of Charity, several agents and nurses, on March 8th consisting of seventy babies. Of these, forty-one went to New Orleans, sixteen to neighboring Louisiana towns, nine to Chicago, and four to Memphis.

In each case, except in New Orleans, the percentage of boys and girls was about equally divided. In New Orleans, however, a strong preference was expressed for baby boys. The letters asked for anything from a "nice child," and "one that can be the sunshine of our home," to babies with black hair and black eyes, and curly hair or red hair.

The homes to which the babies were sent were inspected three times by different persons beforethe babies left New York, and a fourth time by the Sisters of Charity now in New Orleans with their charges. Some of the parents to be expressed a preference for orphans, and others for foundlings, but in no case was the history of the child asked for or submitted. In every case the baby seemed to give satisfaction, and it is believed that the renewed demand for babies in New Orleans was stimulated by international gossip and boasting over last weeks' cargo of infantile sunshine and squalls.

From the south, also, yesterday Mayor Gaynor received a letter asking help in obtaining children.

Two citizens of Holland, Texas wrote requesting him to send them a boy and a girl for adopting. The letter said that the writers understood that there were a number of children in New York without homes, and continued: "There are two of us here that want a child a piece; a bright boy about twelve years of age, and a girl from ten to twelve. I want a girl able to read and write some. We will give them good homes, send them to school, and treat them as well as if they were our own children. If you can get us these children please send them right away." The Mayor declined to make public the names of his correspondents, but said that one was a Baptist clergyman, and the other a farmer.

The New York Times
April 5, 1911

Credit: The New York Times page 6. Foundlings Sent West

FOUNDLINGS SENT WEST
Sixty-six Shipped in a Special Car to Homes of Foster Parents

Sixty-six babies from the New York Foundling Hospital were shipped yesterday to foster parents in the South and West in a special car on the noon train for St. Louis from the Grand Central Station.

The sixty-six foundlings were in charge of two Sisters of Charity and Agent O'Hara, who has been conducting the hospital's semi-annual transcontinental foundling tours for a great many years.

When the foundlings reach St. Louis they will be taken to homes in Union City, Terra Haute, Kansas City and Victoria. The other group will be taken to homes in Arkansas, Oklahoma, Texas, and Louisiana.

The trip is the result of applications for foster children which are constantly coming in to the society from charitable folk in other cities. The homes of the applicants are thoroughly investigated by the agents of the hospital before the applications for the babies are granted. Prospective foster parents this year include two lawyers, two doctors, and many farmers.

The babies wear the same clothes on the trip which they wore on their admission to the hospital, and each carries this letter from Sister Teresa Vincent:

Dear Friend:
Within a week after the reception of the little one will you please fill out the enclosed slip and forward it to us. Please write us yearly, about May 1st, how the little child is progressing, with any items of interest. Wishing you many blessings for your kindness to the 'orphan.'

I am in our dear Lord, yours respectfully,

SISTER TERESA VINCENT
The New York Foundling Hospital

Included with the slip is the blank to be filled out and returned. It requires the name of the child received, the full name of the foster parents, the business of occupation of the foster father, and the full Post Office address.

Since its foundation forty-one years ago, the hospital has provided for 52,673 infants. Last year 500 children were placed in permanent homes with yearly supervision lasting from fifteen to eighteen years. In 1910 there were 1,870 deserted and 850 committed children received.

SIXTY MOTHERLESS BABIES START TO FIND NEW MOTHERS IN THE WEST

Children Leaving the New York Foundling Asylum

Many in Foundling Hospital Since Few Hours After Birth –Fine Homes for Some.

THREE of the CHILDREN

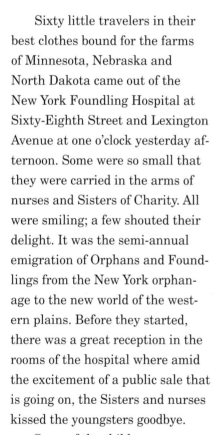

Sixty little travelers in their best clothes bound for the farms of Minnesota, Nebraska and North Dakota came out of the New York Foundling Hospital at Sixty-Eighth Street and Lexington Avenue at one o'clock yesterday afternoon. Some were so small that they were carried in the arms of nurses and Sisters of Charity. All were smiling; a few shouted their delight. It was the semi-annual emigration of Orphans and Foundlings from the New York orphanage to the new world of the western plains. Before they started, there was a great reception in the rooms of the hospital where amid the excitement of a public sale that is going on, the Sisters and nurses kissed the youngsters goodbye.

Some of the children were no more than three years old. Those who could talk plainly proclaimed they were going "to find momma and papa."

For the majority of them, the momma's and papa's to whom they were going were the first they had ever known. Some had been in the hospital since they were brought there a few hours old.

With the warm blessing of Sister Superior Teresa, and into the care of Charles P. O'Hara, and three Sisters of Charity nurses, the party boarded a street car, and went to the Grand Central Station where a special car attached to the 2 o'clock Chicago train known as the "Westerner" awaited them. A crowd watched the youngsters who were carried and laughing, through the waiting rooms to the train.

"These children are going into Western homes, most of them on farms, where babies are greatly longed for," said Sister Teresa, "The persons who have asked for babies have been carefully investigated, and their characters have been certified by clergymen in the neighborhood. At every station where a child is to be placed the new guardian will await the train, and receive the child from the car steps.

"Every year the children will be visited by our agents. When any one who has taken a child proves unworthy the child is taken away. On this trip they are going as far west as Northern Nebraska and some of them to homes where there is wealth and culture. Sometimes the people have lost a beloved child, and sometimes they have never been blessed with children.

"In most cases these little folk will never know they are foundlings. In many cases they are adopted legally, and become the heirs of their adopted parents. Some of our boys sent out this way in years past have become prominent citizens, great lawyers, legislators, and bankers. Only the other day a prominent western lawyer wrote to us that he was making a success of life, and thought we would be glad to hear of it. Bless him, but we were! And who knows but one of these little fellows going out today may be future Presidents bound westward to make their way in the world?"

Minneapolis (Minnesota)
Journal
November 19, 1913
Ccredit: The Minnesota Historical Society

NEW HOMES FOR ORPHANS

One Hundred from New York Distributed in Stearns County, Minnesota Towns

Children from the Foundling getting ready to board an orphan train from Grand Central Railway Station in 1923. They will be accompanied by several Sisters of Charity, nurses, and agents to their new homes in the West.

The New York Foundling Hospital Collection. Al Appleton.

St. Cloud, Minnesota— One hundred orphans from a New York asylum conducted by the Sisters of Charity, arrived here today, and will be delivered to homes which have been provided for them. The orphans will go to homes at Avon, Cold Springs, Holdingford, Freeport, Lake Henry and other places. They range in age from one to four years.

The New York Times
September 28, 1915
Credit: The New York Times page 11. 55 Foundlings Sent West

55 Foundlings Sent West
Girls In Demand by Those Who Will Give Them Homes

Fifty-five foundlings, ranging in age from one to four years, left Grand Central Terminal yesterday morning in a private car for new found homes in the West. It was the latest exodus from the New York Foundling Hospital, on Sixty-Eighth Street, between Lexington and Third Avenues, whose agents have found homes for nearly 20,000 children in the last forty-six years.

There were forty-four girls and eleven boys as it was explained by the Sisters at the home, girl babies are in greater demand. The children were in charge of four nurses, and two Sisters. Beds for them all and food enough for one day were taken on the car.

The babies are going to homes in Minnesota, and the Dakotas. There they will grow up without knowing that they are not the personal children of the foster parents. After three years they may be legally adopted.

The New York Foundling Hospital has about 2,400 inmates, of which 800 are in the hospital, and the others live with families outside.

The Evening World
1918

Credit: The New York Foundling Collection

100 BABIES NEW YORK'S CHRISTMAS GIFT TO CHILD HUNGRY HOMES-SOUTH AND WEST

The New York Foundling Collection

War Has High Demand for Youngsters, Says Head of the Foundling Asylum More Than 1,000 Appeals Received

One hundred Christmas presents, gifts in curls and pinafores, will be dispatched from this city tomorrow to that many homes in the Mississippi Valley, the Southwest, and the far reaches of the Northwest. These presents are just kids, chubby, well-fed and happy for the most part, although there are some in whose eyes is reflected the gaunt spectra of an unprotected past.

The hundred kiddies are the gift of the New York Foundling Asylum to a hundred homes in the West. They will leave here tomorrow on a special train provided by the New York Central. They will journey to St. Paul, Minnesota and once there will separate to go their respective ways. These waifs, human driftwood thrown up by a great city in the ebb tide

of misfortune, are going out in a hundred different directions to bring a Yuletide spirit into a hundred childless homes.

Appeals for Christmas babies have broken all records at the Foundling this year. The Mother Superior, a motherly woman who holds a wonderful spiritual power over her children, told a reporter for The Evening World yesterday that the babies being sent away on Tuesday answered only a small portion of the Christmas demands made upon the institution. "A thousand childless homes are calling for youngsters, and we are able to fill less than one-tenth of the demand," said the Mother Superior. "The war has high demand for babies, and the batch of 100 going away on Tuesday is only a small portion

of what we might send if we were in a position to fill the volume of requests we have received."

The New York Central has provided a special car in a special train for them, and the children will be in charge of five Sisters and several nurses, who will conduct each child to its new home. Most of the children are going to the Middle West, but some will go out as far as Montana and Oregon. One of the children, Stephen Young, will go to Butte, Montana. He seemed delighted with the Western prospect, and let out a real cowboy whoop when an Evening World photographer fired a flashlight taking his picture. The ages of children bound for new homes range from nine months to four years, with boys and girls equally divided.

The New York World
December 11, 1918
Credit: The New York Foundling Collection

Real Fathers and Mothers are Christmas Gifts for These Babies

When a big special drawing room car attached to a fast train pulled out of the Grand Central Terminal yesterday afternoon it had as precious passenger's sixty little children who never knew papa and momma. The principal Christmas gift this year for each child will be a real papa and momma, for the happy little youngsters are on their way to the Far West, where adopted parents await and clasp them to their breasts and welcome them as new members of their families.

Since the first few weeks of their existence the little ones had been under the loving care of the good Sisters of Charity at the New York Foundling Hospital; Sixty-eighth Street and Third Avenue. Yesterday was the first time any of the babies; the oldest had just turned two years, and the youngest not more than nine months; had been outside the institution since their admission. Each child had been abandoned by its mother or father.

Gazing upon these children, who looked more like dolls, ensue the last word in neatness and daintiness. Each child is immaculately clean and dressed in clothing new "from the skin

The New York Foundling Collection

side out" as one of the nurses stated. Who could guess that some of them had been found with life almost extinct in

hallways, waiting rooms of subways, elevated stations, and in numerous 'other places,' even in ash cans.

Cared for 60,000 Children

The New York Foundling Hospital, of which Sister Anna Michella is Sister Superior, has taken in 60,000 children and has placed 22,600 in comfortable homes since its founding in 1869 throughout the country. Yesterday was the first time in more than a year that a band of little children left the institution to have their destinies shaped under the guidance of persons who have been investigated thoroughly by the priest of the parish to which they are sent.

At the sound of a great bell in the main hall of the hospital the sixty children, and their escort of two nuns, three nurses, and

Charles P. O'Hara the agent in charge of transportation and feeding, prepared to leave for the train. Inside the coat of each youngster was their name in embroidered letters. Tacked to the collar was a ribbon on which was printed a number. Some of the ribbons were pink; others were white, blue, yellow and brown. Each color denoted the state to which the little foundlings were going, and the number meant the city where papa and momma waited.

Four are speeding to Montana, five to North Dakota, thirty-eight to Minnesota, twelve to Indiana, and one to Wisconsin. The little traveler to the state of Wisconsin is called Louise, and she was one of the proudest little creatures imaginable. Her pretty brown coat of velvet and cap to match, and little muff that hid her gloved hands was the cause of her pardonable pride. She strutted up and down the hall, and succeeded in finding a prominent place when photographers made pictures.

Of the sixty children, forty were girls many of whom had to be carried to the stages waiting outside the building. At the signal from the Sister Superior the children started for the conveyances, which had been specially heated. A chorus of "Papa! Momma!" went forth from fifty-nine throats, the remaining one saying, "Santa Claus!" much to the merriment of the nuns. Each child was kissed by the Sisters, who later softly wept tears of joy that the children were going to good homes.

Sixty little foreheads were kissed by the big special policeman in gray, Jan Fohey, who for the last fifteen years protected the institution from outside annoyances. Mr. Fohey, who is a retired policeman, is godfather to every child in the hospital, and he is able to call every one by name.

1880s, Seton Hospital Nazareth, established by the New York Foundling Hospital; a summer home along the Hudson River in the lower Bronx, for children with delicate health conditions. Bottom step left stands Sister Mary Rosalie. Top step left stands Sister Bernadette, and to her right stands Sister Teresa Vincent.

The New York Foundling Hospital Collections.

The big policeman carried three children at a time to the stages, and saw that each one was tucked in a robe.

Hospital in Debt

Special individual bedding went with the travelers, and another new outfit of clothing. All this in spite of the fact the New York Foundling Hospital is in debt $100,000 according to the latest report filed with the City of New York by the institution.

Soups, crackers and milk, enough to hold the children's appetites for today, was carried by agent O'Hara, who has made these trips before. He telegraphs ahead to principal cities, and three times a day fresh food is supplied upon arrival of the train.

The New York Foundling Hospital
Date unknown

Credit: The New York Foundling Hospital Collection

Thirty Foundlings Start for New Homes in the West

Thirty children, joyous at the prospect of "a ride on the choo-choo cars," were taken from the New York Foundling Hospital at No. 175 East Sixty-Eighth Street yesterday to begin their journeys to new homes in Indiana and Iowa.

The little ones are going in age from sixteen months to two and half years, and have been adopted. The hospital still has 2,676 foundlings.

St. Paul, (Minnesota) Pioneer
1918

Credit: The Minnesota Historical Society

ST. PAUL, MINNESOTA A CARLOAD OF ORPHANS
Fifty Infant Orphan's Heads of Curly Hair
Bounce in Depot's Murkiness

Little babies,

big babies,

fat babies, too,

Black heads,

brown heads,

red heads a few.

Sisters, brothers,

yes, and cousins,

Babies by the tens

and babies by

the dozens.

A carload consignment of chubby, dimpled little bits of humanity arrived in St. Paul this morning. They are 50 foundling waifs who were brought all the way from the New York Orphan's Foundling asylum to be placed in new homes in the Northwest. Anxiously waiting on the platform as the train drew in were a score of men and women, prospective St. Paul and Minneapolis parents for a dozen of the tiny youngsters.

Station Attachés Amazed

Baggage hustlers, express men, and station attachés at the Union Depot stopped their work to gaze in wonder at the car attached to the train on the St. Paul Road from Chicago. Fifty pairs of baby eyes were peering from the windows of the car into the gloomy smoke soaked atmosphere. Curly hair of brunette, blonde, and auburn, bounced up and down inside. Three nurses and two Sisters from the Home were busy caring for the babies. In the front end of the car, dressed in white coats, caps and mittens, sat the children who were destined to begin life anew in St. Paul, and nearby towns.

Each Babe Numbered

On each shoulder was pinned a bow of ribbon with a number stamped on it. However, the number was merely to facilitate the work of keeping track of the children. They all have names, and the nurses and Sisters do not call them by numbers.

There was a minimum of crying, and lots of laughing and cooing. One real casualty occurred when Margaret's finger accidently wandered into Dorothy's mouth and was bitten, not hard, of course, but sufficient enough to cause an out cry from the owner of the finger.

For months Charles P. O'Hara, agent for the Foundling Home has been traveling through the Northwest seeking homes for the children. Prospective parents were not permitted to go through the car and make a selection. An order is sent in by the new parents.

ORPHANS IN THE NEWS: THE NEW YORK JUVENILE ASYLUM

The New York Times
January 30, 1885

Credit: The New York Times page 8.

Reforming Young Wrong-Doers

Children making shoes as part of the industrial school training at the Juvenile Asylum in New York. Date unknown.

Library of Congress

The New York State House of Refuge opened January 25, 1825 at the intersections of Broadway and Twenty-Third Street operated by the Society of the Reformation of Juvenile Delinquents. Any child in the state convicted of committing a petty crime or for disorderly conduct was sufficient justification for placement in the House of Refuge.

In 1851 the Children's Aid Society built the New York Juvenile Asylum to house children under the age of twelve. In 1875 the Society for the Prevention of Cruelty to Children was formed to protect the rights of children.

By December 31, 1883 there were 923 children in the asylum. Of these, 491 were sent back their parents, 183 indentured in Illinois, 7 indentured near this city, 16 discharged by magistrates, 4 transferred to other facilities, and two released on rights. In 1884, there were 653 children received. Of these, 317 for disobedience and truancy, 15 for pilfering, 35 for vagrancy, 277 for destitution, and 9 for begging.

A large number of children were surrendered to the institution by parents and guardians. The asylum was designed for reaching children who have begun a career of vice receiving on average 800 youth per year. The children were involved in industrial school training involving tailor shops where over 10,000 garments were made in the function of Summer and Winter jackets and trousers, caps and suspenders; in the boys and girls sewing shops clothing is both made and repaired resulting in tens of thousands of articles. In the shoe shop over 1,300 pairs of shoes are made annually, and in the farm and garden department children are educated in the fruits of the earth.

A separate children's court system was designed in 1892 since children were tried in criminal courts to reform their behavior. As the influx of immigrations declined in the 1920s so did the number of children on the streets; eventually laws took the place of protecting the child.

The New York Times
October 5, 1871

*Credit: The New York Times page 8.
New York Juvenile Asylum*

New York Juvenile Asylum

The monthly meeting of the Board of Directors was held on Tuesday evening at the House of Reception, No 61 West Thirteenth Street. Mr. A.R. Wetmore, the President, and Mr. Carpenter, the Superintendent of the Asylum at One Hundred and Seventy-sixth Street near High Bridge, presented a monthly report.

It appeared that 524 boys and 97 girls are now in the institution, all of whom are in good health. During the last month, a company of children was sent west for indenture in the State of Illinois where several hundred wards of the institution are already happily established in good homes. The Board will hold their quarterly meeting at the Asylum on which occasion there will be public exercises by the school, and music by the Asylum's Cornet band composed of twenty-one boys.

@ Bettmann/CORBIS

The New York Juvenile Asylum located at Tenth Avenue and 176th Street was incorporated by a legislative act in 1851. The asylum provided care for children under the age of twelve, and many were sent west on orphan trains. This 1938 photograph depicts a class during Sunday School at the Village.

The New York Times
August 3, 1869

Cedit: The New York Times page 3. Youthful Emigrants for the West

Emigrants For the West

A company of thirty-one boys and girls left this City for Illinois yesterday. They are sent by the New York Juvenile Asylum. Good homes are provided for them among farmers. Every month or two children are sent from the asylum to Illinois, the legislature of that state having passed an act legalizing the indentures of the asylum. The children are indentured until they are of age. The institution has two agents who will receive them in Chicago and procure homes for them. The boys receive $200 when they are of age, and the girls $50. Each child receives two new suits of clothes when the terms of the indentures expire.

LADY LIBERTY

The New Colossus

Not like the brazen giant of Greek fame,
With conquering limbs astride from land to land;
Here at our sea-washed, sunset gate shall stand
A mighty woman with a torch, whose flame
Is the imprisoned lighting, and her name
Mother of Exiles. From her beacon-hand
Glows world-wide welcome; her mild eyes command
The air-bridged harbor that twin cities frame.
"Keep, ancient lands, your storied pomp!" cries she
With silent lips. "Give me your tired, your poor,
Your huddled masses yearning to breathe free,
The wretched refuse of your teeming shore.
Send these, the homeless, tempest -tost to me,
I lift my lamp beside the golden door!"

EMMA LAZARUS (1849-87)

The number of tenements spiraled with
the incursion of immigrats. Elizabeth Street
in New York City 1912.

Lewis Hine Collection

IMMIGRATION

For the immigrants who came to the United States by ship in the late nineteenth and early twentieth centuries, the Statue of Liberty made a permanent impression as the first landmark they saw as they approached their new home. Many people faced long overland journeys, while others stayed in New York, crowding into the Lower East Side of Manhattan and the area known as Five Points. By 1910 more than half a million immigrants were crammed into tenements throughout New York City.

Poverty, disease, destitution, no money, and no work led many to abandon their children to the city streets. The next "leg of the journey" for many children of poor immigrant families arriving in New York became known as "the orphan trains."

RAILROADS TIED TO HISTORY

The history of the railroads is deeply tied to the orphan train era. Railroads remained the most inexpensive way to move numerous children westward from poverty-filled homes, orphanages, poorhouses, and city streets.

By 1860, 30,500 miles of track had been laid. Eleven railroads met in Chicago. The building of the railroads spurred western settlement. In 1862 Congress authorized construction of two railroads to link the Midwest and the West Coast. The Union Pacific extended westward from Nebraska; the Central Pacific reached eastward from the Pacific Ocean. The meeting of the two railroads at Promontory Summit, Utah, in 1869 signaled a new era of western history. By 1870 the trains ran from the East Coast to Omaha, Nebraska.

The New York Central Railroad headquartered in New York served most of the Northeast, including extensive trackage in New York, Pennsylvania, Ohio, Michigan, Indiana, Illinois, and Massachusetts, plus additional lines in the Canadian provinces of Ontario and Quebec. Its primary connections included Chicago and Boston. The train route from New York's Grand Central was almost certainly the New York Central, as the railroad owned the station. Other railroads used the Pennsylvania Station (Penn Station) in New York City beginning in 1910.

The New York Central never went west of Chicago which was the dividing line. Nothing in the East went further west, and nothing in the West went further east. The child's destination determined alternative routes. Children arriving at a Midwest station from New York were oftentimes switched over to another railroad in Chicago or St. Louis as they continued their journey farther west.

An orphan train bound for Texas in 1904.

The Children's Aid Society

BELOW:
Panoramic scene of an
orphan train in Kansas.

The Kansas Historical Society Collection

Grand Central Station, New York City, 1895.
Library of Congress

CHILDREN OF THE TRAIN

An accurate number of children who rode an orphan train from New York, Boston, and other East Coast orphanages migrating to the west will never be completely known, but estimates suggest upward of 250,000 children. Approximately one hundred orphan train riders are still living today. For these "children of the train and their descendants," much information relating to their identities has been lost due to poor recordkeeping at the agencies that handled the adoptions, alteration of factual information, and suppression of details in order to promote a new start.

Joining a new family in the West brought the possibility of a better life than the instability confronted by these children. Many advanced to respectable homes, but others did not and were ill-treated. The placing–out system had its successes and its failures.

The following narratives illustrate a brief biographical portrait of a modest number of orphan train riders from New York. These children of the train commonly grew up with positive character in spite of the adversities they faced. Their stories a legacy of the largest mass migration of children in history, never to be duplicated again.

CHILDREN
OF THE TRAIN

BORN:
Sophia Kaminsky
(variant spellings Kominsky, Komisky, Komesky, Kaminisky, Kamin) on April 22 or 23, 1915, at Villa Avenue, Bronx, New York.

BIOLOGICAL PARENTS:
William Kaminsky and Maria/Merry. One parent was born in Germany in 1896. Maria relinquished her five and a half-month-old infant daughter to the New York Foundling Hospital on October 9, 1915, in very poor health.

FOSTER/ADOPTIVE PARENTS:
Joseph and Mary (Melich) Duda
of 4306 Penn Avenue North, Minneapolis, Minnesota.

FOSTER/ADOPTIVE PARENTS:
Widow Anna Greim of Cass Avenue, Springfield, Minnesota.

FOSTER/ADOPTIVE NAME:
Sophia Greim.

ORPHANAGE:
The New York Foundling Hospital, NYC.

RODE AN ORPHAN TRAIN TO:
Minneapolis, Minnesota, arriving on June 30, 1917, at the age of two and received by Joseph and Mary Duda. Saved from a return trip to New York in January of 1919, four-year-old Sophia was placed in the home of Mrs. Anna Greim. Circumstances with her prior placement proved unsatisfactory.

Sophia married Charles Hillesheim on June 4, 1936, in Springfield, Minnesota, where the couple raised five children. She became a young widow in 1966, raising their children alone after Charlie succumbed to a heart attack.

Sophia married widower Raymond Kral on February 14, 1985, in Sleepy Eye, Minnesota. She became a widow in 2007. In 2009, Sophia is ninety-four years old, very active, and intellectually vibrant.

Four-year-old Sophia's first photo in
Springfield, Minnesota

Eight-year-old Sophia.
Only two childhood pictures exist.

SIGNATURES

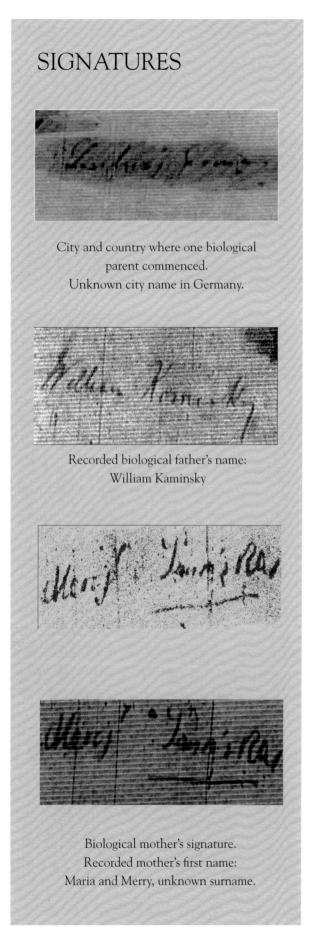

City and country where one biological
parent commenced.
Unknown city name in Germany.

Recorded biological father's name:
William Kaminsky

Biological mother's signature.
Recorded mother's first name:
Maria and Merry, unknown surname.

The marriage of Sophia
Kamin/Kaminsky-Greim
and Charles E. Hillesheim on
June 4, 1936 at St. Raphael's
Church, Springfield, Minnesota.

Sophia Hillesheim-Kral
at her ninetieth birthday
celebration.
"I don't have a birth
certificate, but I'm here."

———————— ⟋⟍ ————————

Where am I going as I climb into the train dressed
brand new,
Leaving behind all I've known at the tender age of two?

Tomorrow is distant I feel forgotten and lost,
The Foundling, a home to me, and in to humanity
I am tossed.

No mother, no father near, to reach out and quell my fears,
No one to hug me or wipe away the tears.

I am "placed-out" to Minnesota, a strange sounding name,
A Sister of Charity holds my hand but it is not the same.

With blowing whistle mysteries lurk,
The train pulls away from Grand Central with a jerk.

With gathering speed the train moves away,
I know not the value of what is lost this day.

The heart of God resides within the orphan's woe,
Whose needs go much deeper than anyone will ever know.

It was God's plan to send you on that train,
To us your children and grandchildren…you were our gain.

BORN:
Giovanni Gauna on December 28, 1909, in Manhattan, New York.

BIOLOGICAL PARENTS:
Maria (Gauna) Mirto.

FOSTER/ADOPTIVE PARENTS:
Frank and Bridget Schutt. Bridget remarried after Frank's death to Anton Thomas in 1920.

FOSTER/ADOPTIVE NAME:
John Thomas.

ORPHANAGE:
The New York Foundling Hospital, NYC.

RODE AN ORPHAN TRAIN TO:
Glen Ullin, North Dakota, arriving on September 18, 1912. An older boy by the name of John Day also came on the same train but went to another relative. John Day did not stay long with his new placement, escaping to the state of Montana.

John Thomas married Ann Holzer September 17, 1935, and the couple raised three children. He worked for a motor company in Bismarck, North Dakota. At the age of eighty-three, John Thomas passed away on August 30, 1993.

John will forever be remembered for his musical talent with his accordion. John's band played for over fifty-four years for area weddings; moreover, his band bill announced, "Dance to the Music of John Thomas." Many fondly remember him as "the accordion guy."

John Thomas

Twelve- year- old John Thomas

John Thomas, fondly rememberd as "the accordion guy."

Three-year-old Helen with her one-year-old step-sister Jeannette and foster parents John and Helen Klonowski.

Six-year-old Victoria's first portrait.

BORN:
Helen Perkins on February 6, 1914, in Tompkinsville, New York.

BIOLOGICAL PARENTS:
Helen Perkins of Massachusetts and Joseph Collins possibly of Virginia.

Helen Koscianski

FOSTER/ADOPTIVE PARENTS:
John and Helen Klonowski of Winona, Minnesota.

FOSTER/ADOPTIVE NAME:
Helen Klonowski.

ORPHANAGE:
The New York Foundling Hospital, NYC.

RODE AN ORPHAN TRAIN TO:
Winona, Minnesota, arriving on June 15, 1916, on the Chicago Moline train at 3:49 A.M. Helen lived with the Klonowski family for twenty-three years. She married Erwin Koscianski on June 19, 1937. Her family consists of nine children, sixteen grandchildren, seventeen great-grandchildren, and one great-great grandchild. As of 2008, ninety-four-year-old Helen Koscianski resides in Winona, Minnesota.

———————————————— ⋘ ————————————————

BORN:
Vittoria Gennaro on April 28, 1912, in New York City.

BIOLOGICAL PARENTS:
Giuseppe and Natala (DiGangi) Gennaro.

FOSTER/ADOPTIVE PARENTS:
Miss Lucy Norton.

Victoria Moe
at her eighty-fifth birthday.

FOSTER/ADOPTIVE NAME:
Victoria Gennaro.

ORPHANAGE:
The New York Foundling Hospital, NYC.

RODE AN ORPHAN TRAIN TO:
Easton, Minnesota, arriving in 1918. Victoria currently resides in Arizona.

BORN:
Mary Sullivan on April 29, 1915, in Manhattan, New York.

BIOLOGICAL PARENTS:
Julia Sullivan and Alex Kalman.

FOSTER/ADOPTIVE PARENTS:
Louis and Elizabeth (Bessie) Bezdicek.

Mary Allendorf

FOSTER/ADOPTIVE NAME:
Mary Bezdicek until the age of eighteen when Mary took her former name in view of a non adoption.

ORPHANAGE:
The New York Foundling Hospital, NYC.

RODE AN ORPHAN TRAIN TO:
Jackson, Minnesota, arriving on June 30, 1917, as a two-year-old. In 1941, Mary married Marshall Allendorf. She was a resident of Arizona for twenty-nine years. As of 2008, Mary is ninety-three years old and resides at an independent living facility in Hopkins, Minnesota.

Five-year-old Mary

BORN:
Marie/Marion Roberts on May 8, 1915, at the Lying-In Hospital Manhattan, New York.

BIOLOGICAL PARENTS:
Marion McCarthy and Walter Roberts.

FOSTER/ADOPTIVE PARENTS:
Dennis and Mary Daly of Eyota, Minnesota.

Mary Anne Carter

FOSTER/ADOPTIVE NAME:
Mary Anne Daly.

ORPHANAGE:
The New York Foundling Hospital, NYC.

RODE AN ORPHAN TRAIN TO:
Rochester, Minnesota, arriving on June 30, 1917, at the age of two. Marie arrived with No. 31 imprinted on a scrap of cloth attached to the left corner of her dress.

Mary married Maynard Carter on December 17, 1945, in Rochester. The couple raised two children while Mary was a secretary for the Olmsted County Extension Service and the Mayo Clinic. At the age of eighty-six, Mary passed away on March 7, 2002.

Two-year-old Mary Anne

CHILDREN OF THE TRAIN

These women rode an orphan train together as children from New York City and arrived in Minnesota on June 30, 1917. The trio were a part of the group described in the accompanying article, "75 Foundlings Off To Find Homes."

The women met for the first time at a Minnesota Orphan Train Reunion in 1994. They reminisced about their homeland and life and discussed their desire to learn more of their ancestry. Many riders did not possess a birth certificate, nor were they able to obtain one, a roadblock that could result in despondency.

Orphan train riders top picture left to right: Sophia (Kaminsky) Hillesheim arrived in Minneapolis, MN, and Mary (Sullivan) Allendorf arrived in Jackson, MN. Bottom picture: Mary (Roberts) Carter arrived in Rochester, MN.

George Abel, Prize Foundling
The New York World, June 27, 1917

75 FOUNDLINGS OFF TO FIND HOMES
Will Meet in West the 'Fathers' and 'Mothers' Whom They Never Have Seen

Seventy-five eager children from the New York Foundling Hospital, accompanied by two Sisters and eight nurses started on the New York Central Railroad at 1 P.M. yesterday for homes selected for them in the West.

All have been told they are going to live with their 'fathers' and 'mothers' and all are happy in the thought of seeing those persons.

Every year the New York Foundling Hospital sends 400 or more children for adoption, and yesterday's lot was a remarkably fine one. Naturally, the youngsters were greatly excited, for they were leaving the only home they had ever known and were going to those before mentioned mysterious 'mothers' and 'fathers' whom they had never seen.

BORN:
Louise Murphy on August 27, 1912, and placed with the New York Foundling Hospital as a lost child from the Cumberland Hospital in Boston, Massachusetts.

BIOLOGICAL PARENTS:
Unknown.

Louise Pfundheller

FOSTER/ADOPTIVE PARENTS:
Friedrich and Ludwica Wild of St. Paul, Minnesota.

FOSTER/ADOPTIVE NAME:
Louise Wild.

ORPHANAGE:
The New York Foundling Hospital, NYC.

RODE AN ORPHAN TRAIN TO:
St. Paul, Minnesota, arriving in 1915 at the age of three. Louise married George Brandin. The couple had three children, raising to adulthood two. Louise became a widow and eventually married Robert Pfundheller. They raised a family of two children.

Louise died at age 96 on June 27, 2009, at her residence in Mitchell Manor in Oak Creek, WI. She was interred in the Spooner Cemetery.

Eight-year-old Louise.

BORN:
Marie Barbara Fields on December 15, 1913, in New York, New York.

BIOLOGICAL PARENTS:
Unknown.

FOSTER/ADOPTIVE PARENTS:
Elizabeth and James Murphy of Minneapolis, Minnesota.

FOSTER/ADOPTIVE NAME:
Marie Barbara Murphy. Marie's adoptive mother was fond of calling her Roseanna. Attempting to tell her adoptive mother her name was Marie, the spoken word was verbalized as "Bowie" which became fixed as a childhood nickname.

ORPHANAGE:
The New York Foundling Hospital, NYC.

RODE AN ORPHAN TRAIN TO:
Minneapolis, Minnesota, arriving in 1915 at the Minneapolis/ St. Paul Milwaukee Road train depot. Marie recalled that another child from the New York Foundling Hospital got off the train with her.

Marie Dorff resides in the Twin Cities metropolitan area of Minnesota.

Marie as a new arrival.

Portrait made soon after of Loretta's arrival at the Gasink family farm.

Loretta and friend at the Gasink farm.

BORN:
Loretta Armstrong on December 25, 1913, in Manhattan, New York. Elizabeth Vangil of 423 East Fifteenth Street found the infant Loretta in the waiting room of the 239th Street Ferry House in front of Greenpoint Avenue at the Greenpoint Station in Brooklyn. A note attached to the baby girl stated she was two weeks old, and

Loretta Kochan

gave her birth name adding that she was Catholic. Matron L. Hayes of the 161st Precinct took the infant to the city nurse on January 7, 1914. Emma LaLellish R.G.N. transported the infant to the New York Foundling Hospital. She was baptized shortly after by Reverend C. Christmas O.P. of St. Vincent Ferrer's Catholic Church at the chapel of the New York Foundling Hospital.

BIOLOGICAL PARENTS:
Unknown.

FOSTER/ADOPTIVE PARENTS:
Henry and Louisa (Schneider) Gasink of New Ulm, Minnesota.

FOSTER/ADOPTIVE NAME:
Loretta Gasink.

ORPHANAGE:
The New York Foundling Hospital, NYC.

RODE AN ORPHAN TRAIN TO:
Wausau, Wisconsin, arriving in 1915 at the age of two. The Gasink family received Loretta and returned to their family home in New Ulm, Minnesota, where their new daughter thrived in a content home.

Loretta married Leo Kochan on November 5, 1940, in New Ulm. The couple relocated to Manitowoc, Wisconsin, and raised a family of five children. At the age of ninety, Loretta Kochan passed away on September 23, 2004, in Manitowoc.

BORN:
Rachel Jones on December 25, 1913, in Saxton, New York.

BIOLOGICAL PARENTS:
Stephen Jones of Hunter, New York and Hannah Cole of Quarryville, New York.

FOSTER/ADOPTIVE PARENTS:
Jans and Jennie (Broesder) Visker of Little Rock, Iowa.

Jennie Kor

FOSTER/ADOPTIVE NAME:
Jennie Visker.

ORPHANAGE:
The Children's Aid Society of New York.

RODE AN ORPHAN TRAIN TO:
Little Rock, Iowa, arriving in 1918 at the age of four.

    Jennie married Henry Kor of Little Rock, Iowa. The couple raised three children while farming in the Marshall, Minnesota area. Jennie was also employed at Marshall Produce. At the age of ninety-one, Jennie passed away on November 16, 2004, at the Morningside Heights Health Care Center in Marshall.

BORN:
Bertha Jones on November 25, 1916, in Saxton, New York.

BIOLOGICAL PARENTS:
Stephen Jones of Hunter, New York and Hannah Cole of Quarryville, New York.

FOSTER/ADOPTIVE PARENTS:
Jans and Jennie (Broesder) Visker of Little Rock, Iowa.

Mary Riemersma

FOSTER/ADOPTIVE NAME:
Mary Visker.

ORPHANAGE:
The Children's Aid Society of New York.

RODE AN ORPHAN TRAIN TO:
Little Rock, Iowa, arriving in 1918 at the age of two.

    Mary married John C. Johnson on November 11, 1944, in Little Rock. The couple raised nine children while farming in Brewster, Minnesota. After John's death, Mary later married Bert Riemersma. At the age of seventy-seven, Mary passed away on January 10, 1993 at the Lake Haven Nursing Home in Worthington, Minnesota.

Sisters on an Orphan Train

Together we rode the train
Sisters and orphans are we,
Confused looks, unspoken pain
Where can momma and papa be?

Placed out to the west
Facing unfamiliar lands,
Bertha nuzzles to Rachel's chest
Anxiously holding hands.

You are more than my sister
You are my best friend,
You are the one that will be there
When my heart needs to mend.

My guiding star
My shining light,
You are my everything
That helps me through the night.

From New York to Iowa we must go
New parents come to greet us,
I love you sister, with you I am whole
Secure within a nucleus.

© 2008 Renée Wendinger

Exchange of market attire to World War I Field Artillery uniform.

Joseph Christopher Pauli

BORN:

Joseph Laudwig Blesch on August 29, 1893, at home on 241 West Thirty-Fifth Street, Manhattan, New York. Attending the birth was midwife Mary Gurning/Guring, who lived at 111 MacDougal or Meadow Street in Manhattan.

BIOLOGICAL PARENTS:

Joseph Blesch from Germany and Anna Noebus from Austria, who were twenty-eight and twenty-three years old, respectively, at the time of Joseph's birth.

FOSTER/ADOPTIVE PARENTS:

Gottlieb and Katharina (Pesch) Pauli.

FOSTER/ADOPTIVE NAME:

Joseph Christopher Pauli.

ORPHANAGE:

The New York Foundling Hospital, NYC.

RODE AN ORPHAN TRAIN TO:

Wadena, Minnesota, arriving in 1899. While the Pauli family was visiting a dry goods store in Wadena, a nun stopped in and asked if anyone would like to adopt a child or two from a New York orphanage. The Pauli's chose Joseph for a son as they already had three daughters.

In the early 1900s the Pauli family moved to Choctaw, Oklahoma. Joseph married Pearl in 1924, and the couple raised a family of four children. At the age of one hundred three, Joseph Pauli passed away in Oklahoma City, Oklahoma.

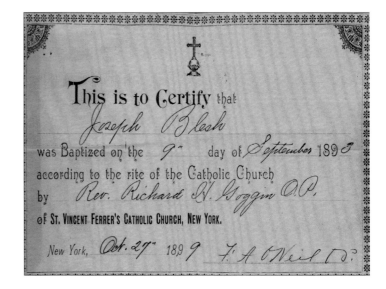

This is to Certify that Joseph Blesh was Baptized on the 9" day of September 1893 according to the rite of the Catholic Church by Rev. Richard H. Goggin O.P. of St. Vincent Ferrer's Catholic Church, New York.

New York, Oct. 27" 1899 F. A O'Neil O.P.

BORN:
Mary Brady on September 4, 1912, in Manhattan, New York. Eleven days after Mary's birth, she was taken to the New York Foundling Hospital, NYC.

Alma Laing

BIOLOGICAL PARENTS:
Mary Brady (mother gave child her given name).

FOSTER/ADOPTIVE PARENTS:
The Herman Frie family of Freeport, Minnesota. The Frie family had received two additional boys from the New York Foundling Hospital prior to Mary. They were ten-year-old Joseph Rose (name changed to Joseph Frie) and Giuseppe Decalogia (name changed to Conrad Frie).

FOSTER/ADOPTIVE NAME:
Alma Frie.

ORPHANAGE:
The New York Foundling Hospital, NYC.

RODE AN ORPHAN TRAIN TO:
Freeport, Minnesota, arriving on November 19, 1913, at the age of thirteen months. Alma lived her life in Freeport, Lake Henry, and St. Cloud, Minnesota.

Alma married Al Laing on June 16, 1931, at Freeport. The couple raised three children. At the age of sixty-six, Alma Laing passed away on March 28, 1979 St. Cloud. She is buried in Freeport.

Two-year-old Alma

Alma's Communion day

Elizabeth Mueck, an accomplished seamstress, sewed exquisite dresses for her four-year-old daughter.

Bernadette Schaefer

BORN:
Bernadette Leblet on December 27, 1921, in Manhattan, New York. Bernadette was baptized at the Church of St. John the Evangelist in New York City on January 19, 1921.

BIOLOGICAL PARENTS:
Alice Leblet from Nanterre, France and Robert Pape. Alice Leblet's father was from Grand Fougeres, France, where he managed the Hotel de France. Alice paid the New York Foundling Hospital for the care of her infant child from April 10, 1922, until January 6, 1923, at which time Bernadette was surrendered to the orphanage.

FOSTER/ADOPTIVE PARENTS:
Elizabeth and Adolph Mueck of Fremont, Nebraska. The Mueck family grew to number eight children when eighteen-month-old Bernadette arrived.

FOSTER/ADOPTIVE NAME:
Bernadette Mueck.

ORPHANAGE:
The New York Foundling Hospital, NYC.

RODE AN ORPHAN TRAIN TO:
Fremont, Nebraska, arriving on June 14, 1923. At the age of eight, Bernadette was legally adopted, and she matured within a favorable home in Lindsey, Nebraska. In her adult life she married Francis Henry Schaefer on October 5, 1943, in Humphrey, Nebraska. The family raised nine children.

Bernadette moved to Minnesota and presently lives in St. Paul. As of 2008, Bernadette is eighty-seven years old and allocates her time speaking to groups about her experiences on the orphan train.

Five-year-old Bernadette and her faithful companion, Shep.

BORN:
William Joseph Williams on August 11, 1910, in Brooklyn, New York, at Kings County Hospital. William was baptized at Holy Cross Church on August 22, 1910, by Reverend John Broderick.

BIOLOGICAL PARENTS:
Julia (Kane) and William Williams.

FOSTER/ADOPTIVE PARENTS:
Widow Magdalena Sand and her brother Bernard Brady.

FOSTER/ADOPTIVE NAME:
William J. Sand.

ORPHANAGE:
The New York Foundling Hospital, NYC.

RODE AN ORPHAN TRAIN TO:
St. Cloud, Minnesota, arriving on December 1, 1913. William married Eleanor Ludenia in 1940. The couple raised a family of six children and enjoyed eleven grandchildren. At the age of seventy-four, William Sand passed away in 1985.

Emily Taylor

BORN:
Emily Repaski on May 23, 1911, in Manhattan, New York.

BIOLOGICAL PARENTS:
Irma Repaski and Joseph Deangelis.

FOSTER/ADOPTIVE PARENTS:
Widow Magdalena Sand and her brother Bernard Brady.

FOSTER/ADOPTIVE NAME:
Emily Sand.

ORPHANAGE:
The New York Foundling Hospital, NYC.

RODE AN ORPHAN TRAIN TO:
St. Cloud, Minnesota, arriving in 1914. Emily married Bert Carey in November of 1934. She was a nurse at Balboa Naval Hospital, serving in the U.S. Navy. In September of 1955, Emily married Charles Taylor. At the age of ninety-two, Emily Taylor passed away in Lemon Grove, California, on July 29, 2003.

Bill, age nine, and Emily, age eight.

Teenagers Emily and Bill Sand

Magdalena Sand and Bernard Brady

Frank Bruggenthies

BORN:
Francis Braun on December 8, 1894, at Old Marion Street Maternity Hospital, located at 139 Second Avenue, New York, New York.

BIOLOGICAL PARENTS:
Unknown.

FOSTER/ADOPTIVE PARENTS:
Christian and Bernadine (Vornbrock) Bruggenthies of Melrose/ St. Rosa, Minnesota.

FOSTER/ADOPTIVE NAME:
Frank Bruggenthies.

ORPHANAGE:
The New York Foundling Hospital, NYC.

RODE AN ORPHAN TRAIN TO:
Melrose, Minnesota, arriving in 1907. Frank was formerly indentured to the Bruggenthies until he reached the age of eighteen. The Bruggenthies also received a girl from the New York Foundling Hospital known as Mary. Francis grew up in a happy family home.

Frank married Mary Toenyan in 1918 in St. Rosa, Minnesota, and raised a family of eight children. The couple farmed and Frank additionally worked in construction. At the age of ninety-two, Frank passed away on November 24, 1987, in Melrose, Minnesota.

Frank Bruggenthies

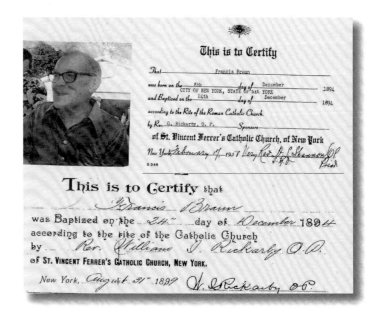

BORN:

In February of 1909. The infant child was found in a vacant lot in Brooklyn, New York. The unnamed baby was taken to local police, and authorities delivered the infant to the city nurse. The Bureau of Child Welfare assigned the baby the name Alice Setley and gave her the birth date of February 2, 1909, since she was gauged to be approximately three weeks old. Alice was assigned a religion and given to the New York Foundling Hospital on February 16, 1909.

Alyce Sullivan

BIOLOGICAL PARENTS:
Unknown.

FOSTER/ADOPTIVE PARENTS:
Nicholas and Mary Theisen of Albany, Minnesota.

FOSTER/ADOPTIVE NAME:
Alyce Theisen (Alice changed the spelling of her name and designated her birthday as February 12, 1909).

ORPHANAGE:
The New York Foundling Hospital, NYC.

RODE AN ORPHAN TRAIN TO:
Albany, Minnesota, arriving on November 21, 1910. Alyce was a proprietor in the restaurant business for many years in Superior, Wisconsin. She married Joseph Sullivan and raised a family of ten sons. At the age of seventy-eight, Alyce passed away in Superior.

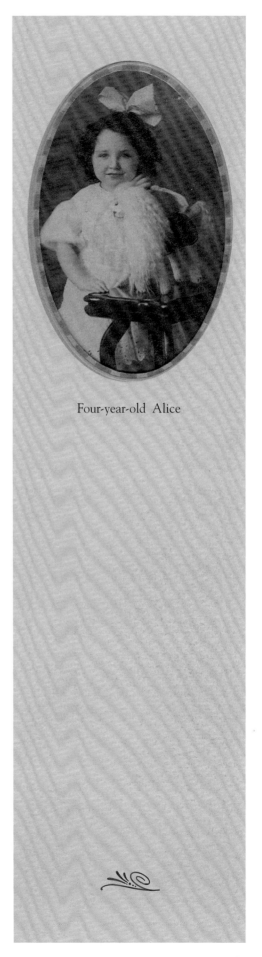

Four-year-old Alice

Anthony Bartishofski

BORN:
Antonio Weidman on August 10, 1911, in Manhattan, New York.

BIOLOGICAL PARENTS:
Anton and Theresa (Wagner) Weidman from Germany.

FOSTER/ADOPTIVE PARENTS:
Martin and Helen Bartishofski of Foley, Minnesota.

FOSTER/ADOPTIVE NAME:
Anthony Weidman. It was not until Anthony was thirty-five years old that the Bartishofskis were encouraged to formally adopt him. As they had no other children, Anthony became their legal heir. In return, Anthony acquired the surname Bartishofski later in life.

ORPHANAGE:
The New York Foundling Hospital, NYC.

RODE AN ORPHAN TRAIN TO:
Foley, Minnesota, arriving in 1914. He later married Violet and served in the 85th Army Infantry during World War II. Anthony resides in Wausau, Wisconsin.

BORN:
Basil on June 17, 1892, in Manhattan, New York.

BIOLOGICAL PARENTS:
Basil's father's surname was Ruki (Japanese), and his mother was a Caucasian American.

FOSTER/ADOPTIVE PARENTS:
Joseph and Sophie Kolosky of Georgetown, Minnesota.

FOSTER/ADOPTIVE NAME:
Basil Kolosky.

ORPHANAGE:
The New York Foundling Hospital, NYC.

RODE AN ORPHAN TRAIN TO:
Georgetown, Minnesota arriving in 1899. As a young man Basil served in the U.S. Army during World War I and subsequently married Eva Lee (the daughter of orphan train rider Harry Lee). Following his wife's passing, Basil transferred to Moorhead, Minnesota.

At the age of ninety, Basil passed away on August 23, 1982, in Georgetown. He was well known as "the photographer" as he captured numerous photo memories.

Basil Kolosky

BORN:
Unnamed on April 25, 1915, at Manhattan General Hospital, located on the corner of East Seventeenth Street and Second Avenue in Manhattan, New York.

BIOLOGICAL PARENTS:
Vague documentation describes the infant's biological mother as a twenty-two-year-old woman living at No. 12 or No. 20 Allen Street in Manhattan, New York. The infant was given up to the New York Foundling Hospital nineteen days after birth and required time at St. John's (the pediatric wing of the hospital).

FOSTER/ADOPTIVE PARENTS:
Julius and Josephine Mary Schroeder.

FOSTER/ADOPTIVE NAME:
Anne G. Schroeder.

ORPHANAGE:
The New York Foundling Hospital, NYC.

RODE AN ORPHAN TRAIN TO:
East Grand Forks, Minnesota, arriving on Columbus Day in 1918. Anne was three years old and attached to her clothing was a tag referencing her as No. 50.

Anne remained single throughout her life and became a working nurse at the Veterans Hospital in St. Cloud, Minnesota. At the age of eighty-two, Anne passed away in St. Cloud.

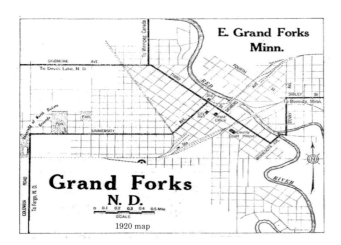

East Grand Forks, Minnesota, was named for its location on the Red River, across from Grand Forks, North Dakota.

Anne G. Schroeder

Anne Schroeder,
age three years eight months.

Mary and companion.

BORN:
Scholastica Scholl at 341 West Broadway, Manhattan, New York, with an Italian ethnicity.

BIOLOGICAL PARENTS:
Calasira Scholl.

FOSTER/ADOPTIVE PARENTS:
The Laible family of Nebraska.

FOSTER/ADOPTIVE NAME:
Mary Laible.

ORPHANAGE:
The New York Foundling Hospital, NYC.

RODE AN ORPHAN TRAIN TO:
Stuart, Nebraska in 1911. Mary married Mark Buscher of Breckenridge, Minnesota, where the couple made their home and raised three children. Mary was the founder of the Orphan Train Riders from New York Reunions surrounding the state of Minnesota. The first reunion was held in 1961 for train riders, descendants, and interested persons. The year 2010 commemorates 50 consecutive reunions. Mary passed away on October 5, 2002.

BORN:
Agnes Chambers on March 1, 1916, at the Lying-In Hospital in Manhattan, New York.

BIOLOGICAL PARENTS:
Tim Finnegan and Mary Chambers from Corcreeny, Northern Ireland.

FOSTER/ADOPTIVE PARENTS:
Harmidas Patnode and Alphonsine (Emard) Patnode of Red Lake Falls, Minnesota.

FOSTER/ADOPTIVE NAME:
Agnes Marie Patnode nicknamed "Pat."

ORPHANAGE:
The New York Foundling Hospital, NYC.

RODE AN ORPHAN TRAIN TO:
Crookston, Minnesota, arriving in 1918. Pat became a schoolteacher for eight grades in a one room schoolhouse before she married Victor Thiessen on August 12, 1939. The couple raised seven sons and one daughter, eventually enjoying twenty-nine grandchildren and thirty-seven great- grandchildren. Pat lives in Becker, Minnesota.

Pat gently holding recently gathered eggs.

BORN:

Gaetano DeLeo on April 20, 1913, in Manhattan, New York.

BIOLOGICAL PARENTS:

Antoinette, a New York opera singer from Florence, Italy and Philipo DeLeo, a coffee plantation owner in Brazil.

FOSTER/ADOPTIVE PARENTS:

Peter and Celia Jutz of New Ulm, Minnesota.

FOSTER/ADOPTIVE NAME:

Joseph J. Jutz. Years later, Gaetano DeLeo amended his name to Guy DeLeo.

ORPHANAGE:

The New York Foundling Hospital, NYC.

RODE AN ORPHAN TRAIN TO:

St. Paul, Minnesota, arriving in 1916. Guy recalled traveling on the train from New York with a nurse he referred to as Hanna. He wore a long dress, and his dark curly locks hung to his shoulders, evoking the image of a diminutive girl. As nurse Hanna delivered Guy to the Jutz family at the train station, the couple stated they wanted a boy. The nurse informed the duo that they would discover they indeed had a boy. The pair immediately bought the child a set of clothes befitting a boy.

Upon returning to New Ulm, Minnesota friends and relatives arrived to see the "boy from the New York Orphanage" and commented, "what a beautiful girl!" Guy's foster mother commenced cutting his beautiful curly locks, yet his attractiveness remained.

Guy graduated from the MacPhail College of Music in 1932 and before long started the Guy DeLeo Dance Band. As a big-name musician and director, he led his sixteen- piece orchestra to become a well- known show and dance band throughout the upper Midwest. In favor of his children, grandchildren, great-grandchildren, and his gift of musical talent, Guy always believed he was the "luckiest man on earth." At the age of seventy-eight, Guy passed away on April 2, 1992, in New Ulm.

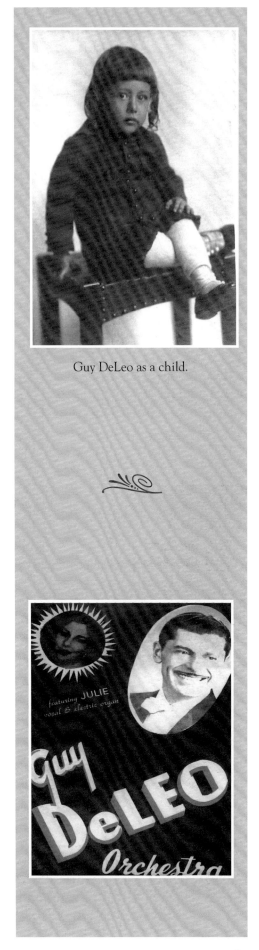

Guy DeLeo as a child.

Emma's first picture
upon arrival by train.

Emma's Communion day

BORN:
Emma Glender on January 24, 1913, at Sloane Hospital in Manhattan, New York.

BIOLOGICAL PARENTS:
Emma Glender (mother gave child her given name) relinquished her two-week-old offspring to the New York Foundling Hospital, on February 5, 1913.

FOSTER/ADOPTIVE PARENTS:
Joseph and Gertrude John of Browerville, Minnesota.

FOSTER/ADOPTIVE NAME:
Emma John.

ORPHANAGE:
The New York Foundling Hospital, NYC.

RODE AN ORPHAN TRAIN TO:
Sauk Centre, Minnesota, arriving on June 19, 1914, at the age of seventeen months. Emma married Rudy Biermaier in Browerville, Minnesota on November 22, 1932. The couple farmed and raised a family of twelve children. At the age of fifty-nine, Emma Biermaier passed away on March 25, 1972, in Browerville.

Emma and Rudy Biermaier

BORN:
Edith Peterson on January 16, 1912, in Manhattan, New York.

BIOLOGICAL PARENTS:
Rebecca Schmidt and Magnus Peterson. Magnus passed away at the age of twenty-eight, six months before Edith was born, leaving twenty-six-year-old Rebecca with two children.

FOSTER/ADOPTIVE PARENTS:
John and Mary Bieganek and Joseph and Rose Bieganek of Avon, Minnesota.

FOSTER/ADOPTIVE NAME:
Edith Bieganek.

ORPHANAGE:
The New York Foundling Hospital, NYC.

RODE AN ORPHAN TRAIN TO:
Avon, Minnesota, arriving on November 29, 1913, at the age of two. Pinned to Edith's coat was number 41, matching the paperwork of John and Mary Bieganek. When Edith turned four years old, Mary died and John moved away to a new town. One of the couple's sons, Joseph, and his wife, Rose, accepted Edith as their own child.

In 1929, the last year the orphan trains carried children to new homes in the West, Edith joined the convent and became Sister Justina Bieganek. She resides at the St. Francis Convent Center in Little Falls, Minnesota. Learning of the orphan train reunions held in Minnesota, Sister attended and met others who shared the same experiences. Little Falls has hosted reunions for twenty-five years, supervised by ninety-six year-old Sister Justina.

The wedding of Joseph and Rose Bieganek with seven-year-old Edith standing center. John Kurtz, a brother to Joseph, was best man. Helen Deering, a sister to Rose, was maid of honor. Circa 1920.

At the summer 2000 reunion of orphan train riders celebration in New York City, Sister Justina Bieganek reflected upon the replica of the original cradle that once stood in the vestibule of the Foundling Hospital, where mothers abandoned their babies.

Rose Ringsmuth with eleven of her thirteen grandchildren.

The extended Thelen family in front of their home in Stearns County, Minnesota.

Back row from left to right: Mother-Mary Ann Thelen, John's wife Kate with son Hubert, Peter Thelen, Nick Jones, Hubert Thelen, Tony Thelen, Henry Thelen, John Thelen, Mike Thelen, Father-Matt Thelen, and Joseph Thelen.
Front row from left to right: Sr. Salone Veronica, six-year-old Rose, John's son Joe, John's son Mike, Bill Thelen, Besseman, Nick Thelen, and John's son Matt.

BORN:
Rose Garmon/Gorman on October 11, 1896.

BIOLOGICAL PARENTS:
Rose's mother was of German heritage and brought her infant daughter to the New York Foundling Hospital on October 23, 1896, at 2:45 p.m.

FOSTER/ADOPTIVE PARENTS:
Sebastian Wimmer of Albany, Minnesota. Rose was later placed with the Mathias and Mary Ann (Wagner) Thelen family of Stearns County, where she was raised with seven brothers. When Mary Ann Thelen passed away in 1929, her brother Henry received care of Rose.

FOSTER/ADOPTIVE NAME:
Rose Thelen.

ORPHANAGE:
The Mothers and Babies Hospital, New York, New York.

RODE AN ORPHAN TRAIN TO:
St. Cloud, Minnesota, in 1899. Rose married Mathias Ringsmuth on June 26, 1923, in Freeport, Minnesota. Just before Rose's ninety-sixth birthday, she passed away on October 4, 1992, in Waite Park, Minnesota.

BORN:
Frances Fager in 1898 in New York, New York.

BIOLOGICAL PARENTS:
Unknown.

Frances Wodarck

FOSTER/ADOPTIVE PARENTS:
Joseph and Frances Puchalla of Royalton, Minnesota.

FOSTER/ADOPTIVE NAME:
Frances Puchalla.

RODE AN ORPHAN TRAIN TO:
Royalton, Minnesota, arriving in 1901. Frances married Stanley Wodarck in Little Falls, Minnesota. The couple raised nine children and enjoyed fifteen grandchildren and sixteen great-grandchildren. At the age of ninety-eight, Frances passed away on June 18, 1996, in Brooklyn Park, Minnesota.

———

BORN:
Laura Martin on May 6, 1909, in Manhattan, New York.

BIOLOGICAL PARENTS:
Lizzie Martin.

FOSTER/ADOPTIVE PARENTS:
Thomas and Mary Carlin of Clear Lake, Minnesota.

FOSTER/ADOPTIVE NAME:
Laura Carlin.

ORPHANAGE:
The New York Foundling Hospital, NYC.

RODE AN ORPHAN TRAIN TO:
Clear Lake, Minnesota, arriving in 1912, as a two-year-old.
Laura married Ole Norden on April 13, 1926, in St. Paul, Minnesota, and spent twenty years working for the St. Cloud, Minnesota, Obstetrics Department. At the age of ninety-eight, Laura passed away on August 31, 2007, in Sauk Rapids, Minnesota.

Frances Wodarck

Laura Norden displaying her two-year-old portrait.

Harry Harrison Lee

BORN:
Harry Lee on January 8, 1875, in New York.

BIOLOGICAL PARENTS:
Rosa Lee.

FOSTER/ADOPTIVE PARENTS:
Hans C. Ihlen from Ihlen, Minnesota.

FOSTER/ADOPTIVE NAME:
Harry Lee.

ORPHANAGE:
Harry progressed through three orphanages in New York City: the Nursery and Child's Hospital on Fifty-First Street and Lexington Avenue, the Nursery and Child's Hospital on Staten Island, and the New York Children's Aid Society.

RODE AN ORPHAN TRAIN TO:
Pipestone, Minnesota, arriving on June 12, 1883, at the age of eight and half years. Harry and the accompanying children on the train were under the attention of agent J. Mathew's Company of the New York Children's Aid Society.

Harry proceeded to Sherburn, Minnesota, in 1893, and was a salesman for A.L. Ward and International Harvester Implement Company. He married Elizabeth Ott on November 4, 1908. Harry labored as a boiler inspector for the State Industrial Commission retiring in 1938. The couple nurtured a family of four children. Their only daughter, Eva, married Basil R. Kolosky, who was an orphan train rider from New York. At the age of eighty-three, Harry Lee passed away on November 18, 1958, in Sherburn.

Harry Harrison Lee

BORN:
Gretchen Mittag on March 8, 1915, in Manhattan, New York.

BIOLOGICAL PARENTS:
Unknown.

FOSTER/ADOPTIVE PARENTS:
Louis and Norine Busch of Howells, Nebraska.

FOSTER/ADOPTIVE NAME:
Margaret Mary Busch, nicknamed Marge.

ORPHANAGE:
The New York Foundling Hospital, NYC.

RODE AN ORPHAN TRAIN TO:
Missouri Valley, Nebraska, arriving in 1917 at the age of fifteen months. The Busch family adopted a boy from the New York Foundling Hospital four years prior to Gretchen's arrival, and they wanted to add a girl to their family unit. Mrs. Busch was an adoptee from Aspen, Colorado.

Marge married Alfred LaMoure in Omaha, Nebraska, on October 2, 1943. Later, the twosome moved to Minnesota and raised a family of five. In 1999 at the age of eighty-four, Marge LaMoure passed away in St. Paul, Minnesota.

Margaret Mary, age two, in Howells, Nebraska, September 1917.

First Communion day for ten-year-old Marge in Dodge, Nebraska, May 1925.

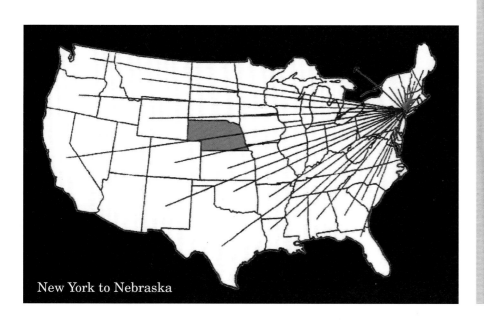

New York to Nebraska

Margaret Mary Busch with her adoptive parents Louis and Norine Busch and adoptive brother Raymond Busch in Howells, Nebraska, July 1917.

Anne's earliest picture.

Anne (center) with friends.

Mary Lamm, orphan train rider
and mother of orphan train rider
Anne Schrankler.

BORN:
Anna Haberbosh on January 12, 1909,
on Forty-Seventh Street in Manhattan,
New York.

Anne Schrankler

BIOLOGICAL PARENTS:
Unknown, but orphanage records state
Ann's birth mother came to the New York
Foundling Hospital every day for one year
to nurse her infant before surrendering her.

FOSTER/ADOPTIVE PARENTS:
Wendell and Mary Lamm of Madelia, Minnesota.

FOSTER/ADOPTIVE NAME:
Anne Lamm.

ORPHANAGE:
The New York Foundling Hospital, NYC.

RODE AN ORPHAN TRAIN TO:
Mankato, Minnesota, arriving on November 21, 1910, at
twenty-two months of age. Anne wore the number 19 imprinted upon a pink ribbon (the color pink designated this child's
state destination was Minnesota) attached to the lapel of her
coat. Anne's adoptive mother, Mary Lamm, also came from
the New York Foundling Hospital as an orphan train rider.
Mary Lamm was born in 1883 as Mary Fitzgerald and lived
with various families along the Canadian border before moving to Madelia, Minnesota, after she married Wendell Lamm.
Mary passed away in 1956, but before her death she pulled
Anne close to her and whispered, "What would I ever have
done without you." Words spoken from the heart of a genuine
mother's love.

Anne married Floyd Schrankler on September 2, 1930. As
of 2008, Anne is ninety-nine years old and resides in a senior
living facility in Woodbury, Minnesota.

BORN:

John M. Arsers in 1865, northern Italy. John remembered his mother's funeral, and when his father remarried, John's stepmother treated him harshly. Someone took John from his home in Italy and put him on a sailboat bound for Paris, France. While in Paris, John played the triangle on the street for money. In 1875 he was put on a steamship with a group of children destined for the United States. He arrived at Castle Garden, located on the southern tip of Manhattan. Before long he was playing music, begging on the streets, and sleeping in apartment doorways and on steps in New York City. Ultimately, John was taken to a place for lost people, but no one claimed him. He was transported to the Children's Aid Society, where Mr. Trout, an agent, took care of John and gave him a new set of clothes but kept his triangle.

John spent a trivial amount of time at the Brace Farm School, and before long he was informed he was going on a trip with other children west. He took into account his position on a train with six boys and a baby girl. He remembered crossing the Niagara River and stopping to see Niagara Falls. The train took him as far as Chicago, where the children switched trains to continue their journeys further west.

FOSTER/ADOPTIVE PARENTS:
Mr. and Mrs. Orin Mildrum of Cresco/Riceville, Iowa.

FOSTER/ADOPTIVE NAME:
John M. Arsers.

ORPHANAGE:
The Children's Aid Society of New York.

RODE AN ORPHAN TRAIN TO:
Riceville, Iowa arriving in 1870, at the age of five. Orin Mildrum's nephew gave John a cornet, and before long he could play several tunes. John went to school and became a skilled tinsmith and constituent of the Osage Iowa Cornet Band. In the spring of 1886, John became director and teacher of the cornet bands in Iowa and Minnesota.

In 1891, John married Sophie Hughes in Osage. The couple raised a family of seven children, spending a number of years between Iowa and Minnesota. At the age of seventy-six, John Arsers passed away in May of 1941, in Osage, where he was widely known as one of the last old time bandmasters.

ARSERS FAMILY
Back row left to right: Linton, Bess, Ida, and Clarence. Front row left to right: Mother-Sophie, Earl, Father-John Arsers, and Ethel.

Italian boy playing the "steel." The triangle is a percussion instrument struck with a wand (or beater). Its tinkling sound is an indefinite pitch, therefore blending with any harmonies an orchestra produces.

Dorling Kindersley Images London, UK.

CHILD ACTRESS REMEMBERS ORPHANS

Baby Peggy celebrating her fifth birthday with the orphans of the New York Foundling Hospital in 1923.

Diana Serra Cary Collection

"Baby Peggy" Jean Montgomery was one of three American child stars of the Hollywood silent movie era in the company of Jackie Coogan and Baby Marie. Discovered at a young age while visiting California's Century Studios on Sunset Boulevard in Hollywood, Peggy went on to stardom. Unfortunately, in later years her dynasty was squandered. Peggy strived, attained, and accomplished her ambition to become a self-made writer and historian. Today she is known as Diana Serra Cary.

As Diana related to this author:

"For decades I have wondered if any of the orphans whose paths I crossed that day in the fall of 1923 survived to tell the tale. The occasion of my visit to the New York Foundling Hospital orphanage was my own fifth birthday. As the world's most famous female rival to Jackie Coogan's male child star image, I was expected to tour New York City. Aside from being given the Key to the City, I visited a Jewish Orphanage, the New York Foundling Hospital, a couple of children's hospitals; appeared on stage at the Immendous of the Hippodrome Theatre; and I sold a new Baby Peggy doll at Gimbels all in one day.

"At the New York Foundling Hospital I was bringing an untouched layer of my five-layer birthday cake, the top of which I had just cut before five hundred members of the National Press and celebrities of the film industry in the ballroom of the Biltmore Hotel announcing a new million-dollar picture contract. It must have been surreal for a child at that orphanage to try to imagine being a movie star at five years of age. While I was standing on the chair cutting the cake, my sister Louise, seated facing me across the table, and I were wondering about those poor children. Even at the age of five, I was sensitive to the situation and wondered if the children would envy and hate me or like me for having brought the cake. I had never been confronted by dozens of orphans in my life until that shockingly, unexpected moment. I am happy that many of them went on to happy and fulfilling lives."

– Diana Serra Cary (Baby Peggy)

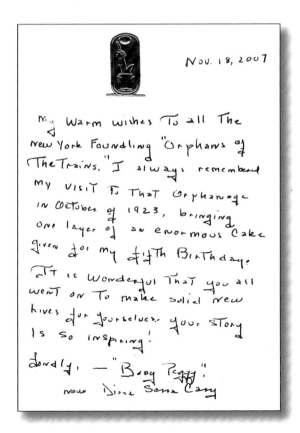

Nov. 18, 2007

My Warm wishes To all The New York Foundling "Orphans of The Trains." I always remember my visit To That Orphanage in October of 1923, bringing one layer of an enormous Cake given for my fifth Birthday. It is Wonderful That you all went on To make solid new lives for yourselves. Your story Is so inspiring!

fondly, – "Baby Peggy" now Diana Serra Cary

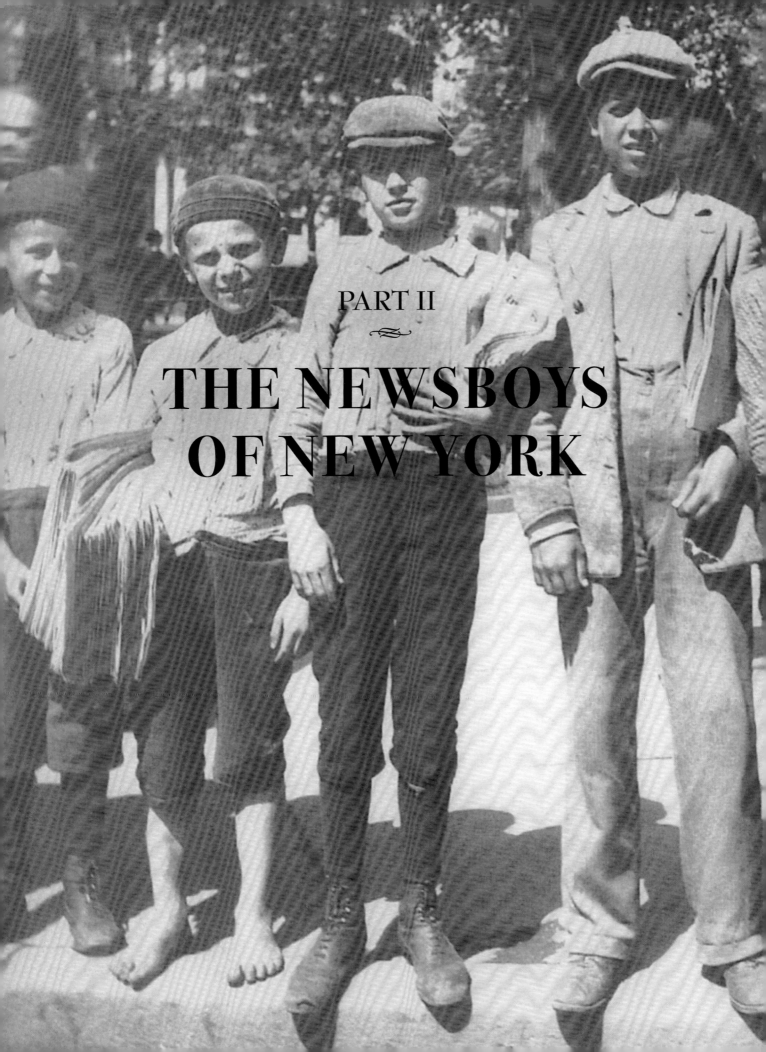

PART II

THE NEWSBOYS
OF NEW YORK

Bound for Missouri in 1908.
The Children's Aid Society Collection

INAUGURATION
OF A NEWSBOY

The first organized effort to help the homeless newsboys was made in 1853, when Charles Loring Brace, a Protestant minister, started a newsboys' lodging home and founded the Children's Aid Society. The society was responsible for placing out newsboys, bootblacks, and children of the street on orphan trains headed west, where they found new family homes. Decisions to go west, stay in New York, or move to an alternative East Coast location were made by the society and the child. The children were called orphans, yet many had living relatives. Once a child departed on the train, neither parent nor child knew how to find each other. Others were orphans, "half" orphans and neglected children abandoned on the city streets.

This section is dedicated to the newsboys, bootblacks, and children of the street. The newsboys not only sold the news, they were very often a part of the news. On the following pages, you'll meet "the newsboys of New York" and discover their link to the orphan trains.

The newsboy.
Library of Congress

NEWSPAPER CHRONICLES

Johann Gutenberg developed a printing method by means of arranging and rearranging stamps displaying the letters of the alphabet. His design became known as the Gutenberg Press. Later, printing machines pressed a blank page against a flat bed of type. A rule placed between every column bound the type together when the press was running. The stereotype rotary press used the bed of type to create a mold by means of pouring molten metal over a mold and a metal plate, bending it into a cylinder. The cylinder was able to withstand the stresses of printing without falling apart. The development of continuous rolls of paper enhanced the original Gutenberg Press in the early 1800s, as did the steam-powered press which used iron instead of wood for construction. The added efficiency of printing resulted in reasonable pricing of printed materials; therefore the "penny press" was accredited as the first true mass medium. The phrase originated when newspaperman Benjamin Day dropped the price of his New York Sun paper to a penny per copy in 1833. It became the first successful penny newspaper and the first newspaper hawked by newsboys on the streets of the city, though initially that honor had belonged to Horace Greeley.

William Randolph Hearst and Joseph Pulitzer each owned newspapers in New York City. Hearst's Journal and Pulitzer's New York World embraced sensationalized reporting recognized as "yellow journalism." Competition between the two newspapers steadily grew, leading to a circulation war. Hearst's presence on New York's "Newspaper Row," a street lined with newspaper buildings, soon created immense competition among the editors of more than fifty dailies. The competitive atmosphere gave birth to "newsboys," and thousands of homeless children tried to earn living selling newspapers. Newspaper Row, also known as Printing House Square, was the newsboy's headquarters, the site of New York's great newspapers.

Two hundred and thirty-four newspapers flourished during the Industrial Revolution, and with the growth of newspapers, interest in the news expanded. As immigration surged during the last half of the nineteenth century, many immigrants published newspapers in their native languages to cater to their comrades. The New York Herald (1835) covered regular beats, spot news, and business including Wall Street. The New York Times (1851) established the principle of balancing reporting with high-quality writing. The New York Tribune (1861) shipped to other large cities and gained national prominence.

In 1886, the Tribune began using the Linotype machine, which offered increased speed in printing. Soon weeklies gave way to dailies, and investigative reporting gave rise to alternative weekly newspapers.

A newsboy at the Duane Street Lodge House in New York City, 1899.

Jacob Riis Collection. Library of Congress.

Printing House Square, 1865. The New York Times is on the right and the Tribune to its left.

THE QUINTESSENCE OF A NEWSBOY

The New York Times
March 12, 1853

Credit: The New York Times page 3.
Character reference: Charles Loring Brace's
Walks Among the New York Poor 1853-54

Park Row newsies in 1910, New York City.
Lewis Hine Collection. Library of Congress.

Standing alone, peddling and bargaining about the city streets on which his very bread and butter depends, the newsboy in the city of New York in the mid 1850s, represents American Independence. When other children were in schools or on playgrounds, he was estimating debit and credit, setting aside enough capital for tomorrow, and elbowing his way through crowds to sell his goods at the best possible rate. He was a 'man' in business when his mates in better classes were engaged in recreation. In a business in which bankruptcy was not an easy relief from obligations, but involved gnawing hunger, and a chance of facing the prison cell. By occupation they were newsboys, but were growing up in a vagrant mode of poverty life.

The newsboy spends most of his young life learning self-help skills. Rags and patches dominate his clothing, revealing fragments of bare skin. Some wear visorless caps and hats that are soft and limp falling over their eyes. Their hair is of all lengths but most wear them short and cropped, with a clean shave from a neighboring barber who charges them three cents a cut. He sleeps where he can find a place-- in charcoal boxes, in hay barges, in printing home alleys, deserted cellars and out buildings, around steam gratings, or in courts behind newspaper offices. If necessary he can live on sixpence a day, but he often earns four to six shillings [a pence is a penny, and a shilling twelve pennies], sometimes working a Sunday to bring in two to three dollars. He puts enough away deep into his pocket to start the next day; the rest goes toward anything that is fitting to his imagination. He is often seen around midnight coming from theatres having a meal in the coffee and cake cellars where many gather, taking their coffee at three cents a cup and biscuit, or lighting their cigarettes and cigars talking over the play. They indulge in gambling activity, or go to the races. He remains indifferent to the world, as long as missionaries and the police leave him alone.

The newsboy is sharp, and he will sometimes cheat strangers as he knows a "green one" from an "old one," and he has the capacity for making old papers look new. He is rough too. The kicks and scuffs of his life have not tended to soften him, and the world has not been so kind to him that he feels an impulse to render kindness in return. Churches and schools he knows nothing of because he was never given the chance; yet he exhibits kind traits helping others when his last penny is shared with a comrade.

Distinct classes among themselves are these boys. They eat, sleep, and make their living as long as people buy their papers and they haven't been stuck [left holding unsold papers]. The best paper to sell in the newsboy's opinion was the

Herald and sometimes Barnum's. Proceeds from the Tribune, The Times, and Herald could make him a twenty-five percent profit buying papers at a cent and a half apiece; the Sun's earnings could pull in thirty percent by the buying quantity of papers at seventy cents a hundred. No trust is given. Some of the older boys, or keepers of the stands, occasionally advance papers to others.

The average age of the newsboy, and a small number of girls, ranged between six and fifteen. Each newsboy has his own beat shouting out the daily headlines, and if one invades the range of another he is well beaten. An average boy will make sixty-two cents to one dollar a day, but if the news is interesting such as an execution in the city or a revolution in another country, the newsboy, or newsie as he is identified, will raise his earnings toward two and three dollars. When a steamer's arrival is announced the excitement of borrowing, lending, and ordering, is given by the older boys who buy up several thousand papers, and resell them. The boys are very shrewd in their business, and seldom get stuck. If he can't read, he asks if any grand accident or news is on hand, and buys his papers accordingly. After every successful "Extra," he is buying something for his needs. The life of the newsboy was tough. In many cases these boys and girls needed to sell papers to buy food, and survive. Fellow newsies formed their own families, though not all were parentless. Some had families and homes, but the lure of hanging out on the busy streets also drew the boys to the work.

Union Square bootblack in 1910, New York City.

Lewis Hine Collection. Library of Congress.

Newsboys waiting for fight 'Extras' after 10 pm in Times Square, New York City 1910.

Lewis Hine Collection. Library of Congress.

BOOTBLACKS

The New York Times
August 17, 1879

*Credit: The New York Times page 5.
Out Among the Newsboys and a Little
Conversation with the Bootblacks*

Twelve-year-old bootblack at his Bowling Green Station, New York City, 1924.
Lewis Hine Collection. Library of Congress.

The Bootblacks rank next to the newsboys, though some carrying on both activities at different hours of the day. Commonly, they range in age from ten through sixteen. They provide themselves with a bootblack kit consisting of a box, paste and brushes. They are sharp and quick witted boys with varied bad habits. They are easy prey to fall into criminal hands, and burglars make use of them to enter dwellings and stores to open doors from the inside.

The bootblacks are said to initiate a confraternity with fixed laws. They have a 'captain,' who as chief of the order, pockets a two dollar fee from any member violating the rules of the society. The fixed rules of blacking a pair of boots or shoes remains at ten cents, the captain punishes anyone who works for less, however a sum that is given in excess of this price is collected. Those that profess to the society never reveal their transactions or places of meeting, as a large part of the earnings is spent on tobacco and liquors. They are regular patrons of the Bowery Theater, and low class concert halls.

On the corner of Frankfort Street one would find a collection of bootblacks eager for business as the newsboys haunt the lamp post and corner steps, from early morning till later in the evening, dressed in all the finery that Chatham Street, and back doors will give up to them. Seven lads take up this area all wearing flat bright blue flannel caps. When a Times reporter inquired as to why the blue caps the answer came as, "Steve Brodie." Steve Brodie was the Napoleon of the newsboys and the George Washington of when he walked in Gilmore's Garden against professional pedestrians. "Steve Brodie wears one so we all wear one and they is cheap!" the boys announced. Rumor has it that Brodie was prosperous, and moved on with his riches to Philadelphia.

The New York Times
August 17, 1879

Credit: The New York Times page 5. Out Among the Newsboys and a Little Conversation with the Bootblacks

New York Bowery bootblack in 1910, New York City.

Lewis Hine Collection. Library of Congress.

The bootblacks took up the area along Frankfort Street for a long time, and kept others away from their territory. One young chap held, "Last week a big fella from Boston came on here. He told he couldn't make a livin there because the boys has to pay half they make to the boss blacker who charges 'em, so he was goin to black in New York." The boy from Boston settled down on their corner, and the regular boys didn't like it. They talked it over, and went to him and said, "Look a here young fella, you'd better move on. You can't black no more boots on this corner. He just laughed, and says how he paralyzed a gang just afore he left Boston, and he'd do the same to us. So the regulars all came over to him and took him in hand. He was so big, but we licked him well. Soon after I met the Boston boy in City Hall Park. He was doin fine, and said it was fair enough," alleged one bootblack.

As the boy continued his conversation with the Times reporter, "Smoke? Yes I smoke, and I'll have to trouble you for a light." Bootblacks don't make a great deal of money as there are many of them and as the bootblacks say, "Eyetalian cheap labor gives a hard pull. There something, and then his box aint doin nothin, and he lends it to some boy what aint got any box, and the boy has to give him half. So then boys make fifty cents if that."

This blue cap lived at the Newsboy's House and continued putting his brushes away saying, "Supper is six cents, breakfast six cents, and lodging six cents if we get in afore nine o'clock. After nine it's seven cents, and past ten it's eleven cents. Dinner is twenty cents, but we generally eat somewhere outside for fifteen or twenty cents." One young lad was not pleased with the Newsboy's Lodging Home. "Don't you see how thin and pale the boys is all lookin?" he said. "Some of 'em is jist about dead, and it's all because they don't git enough to eat. They don't get nothin but bread and molasses, and that aint nothing to live on. Why, there was one fella went to the doctor said he had consumption from eatin that bread molasses. I use to live there, but don't no more. Somebody throwed stones at the Superintendent and they said it was me, and turned me out. It wasn't me! So now I'm over in the Brooklyn Lodging House, that's not so big, but we don't have to eat bread and molasses."

An inquiry followed proving this boy's basis was unfounded as the other newsies were unanimous in saying the fare was good. The worst complaint the boys all had was that someone with a strap goes around in the morning among the boys who are not inclined to get up at a reasonable hour, and a switch is laid upon the bare legs he finds.

The seven on this street corner make up a minor part of the bootblacks and newsboys. Within a circle of a half a mile diameter surrounding City Hall there are at least 250 bootblacks, and countless newsboys, as their numbers change throughout the day. The iron gratings on the margin of Printing House Square with warm air coming up from the engines beneath and sometimes steam are favorite lodging places for many during the winter months; those places are deserted in the summertime when the boys can make themselves comfortable on any convenient step or sidewalk.

The newsboys, the bootblacks, the boys who run errands, hold horses, pitch pennies, sleep in barrels and steal their bread, are the same boys who know more at the age of twelve than most men's boys know at twenty. Upon the age of seventeen or eighteen the bootblack abandons the calling, and is unfit for any other employment by reason of laziness or want of skill. He becomes a loafer and a bummer, or a criminal. The Children's Aid Society has saved many from dejected lives, and has enabled them to become respectable and useful members of society.

Greek bootblacks in 1906,
New York City.

Lewis Hine Collection.
Courtesy George Eastman House.

The New York Times
June 15, 1907

Credit: The New York Times page 2. City Hall Park Stands Must Go

Ten-year-old shiner in 1924, Hartford, Connecticut.

Lewis Hine Collection. Library of Congress.

Commissioner Moses Herman issued an order that all the news stands and bootblacks are to go around City Hall Park. Sorrowed by the order was "Mike the Newsy," "Old Joe," "The Count," and scores of others. The latecomers are the blame, but those who have had stands in the park before Mayor Strong's time must get out and hustle for new sites of business.

In the small park there are over fifty news and about thirty bootblack stands. Most of them are put up when nobody's looking, and 'the lane' used as a straight walk extending from Warren Street to the Brooklyn Bridge inhabited by shoe polishers and news dealers, that the beauty of the park was marred blocking the progress of the 5 o'clock crowd.

"Hully gee!" said Mike. "Dey can't git me out o' dis park. Say, let 'em take d'stand. I'll put me poipers under me arm, and sell 'em dat way. Me bum arm'll have to work, dats all." Mike had a withered arm, and it was a park sight to see him sell papers to a customer, and make change for another at the same time with one hand.

"The Count" was a bootblack who did a great deal of business on rainy days commented, "Hugh gotta maka da live. Some day maka tree dolla eacha chair, two chair sixa dolla. I find a notha place." The news dealers blamed the bootblacks for the stand explosion. When there were one or two bootblack stands in the area there was no trouble, and business was good for everyone, but the "shiners" returned with constructed soap boxes, a bit of dirty carpet, and an old wooden chair to set up stands. Underneath the over head entrance to the Brooklyn Bridge rested a flower stand and a news depot, where proprietors paid the city each year. Across the sidewalk at the park railing were scores of news stands whose owners paid no rent which resulted in cut profits.

A 1927 New York Times article acknowledged that twenty-nine news dealers and bootblacks held concessions for operating stands at strategic points in the areas bound by Broadway, Park Row, Chambers and Mail Streets. Official notices were given cancelling their permits, and the Bureau of Encumbrances sent trucks to pick up the stands from the park. Mayor Walker was called upon to hear the grievances, and later affirmed that the eviction of the stands and bootblacks was "an out rage" immediately directing cancellation. The Mayor considered the newsies and bootblacks performed a real public service and would not tolerate such an order. When the assistant to the Mayor delivered the news to the Commissioner he told him, "I am instructed to tell you that you are to revoke your revocation of permits at once, and that if trucks start to remove any of these news stands, you are to go out upon the first truck." The stands remained.

RIGHT:
Newsies and bootblacks shooting craps in 1910, New York City.
Lewis Hine Collection.

Courtesy George Eastman House.

Mulberry Street area of New York City in 1890. Jacob Riis Collection.
Courtesy Museum of the City of New York.

STREET BOYS

Ten thousand vagrant children lived in the city in eleven wards, and over three thousand children, of whom two thousand were girls between the ages of eight and sixteen, were regularly trained to theft. New York was unable to deal effectively with the tides of immigration that tripled the city's population. Industrialization and the Civil War induced adversity and encouraged epidemics such as cholera, typhus, yellow fever, trachoma [a contagious eye disease], and favus [a chronic disease of the scalp]. Delinquents, prostitutes, beggars, and drunkards dwelled in contaminated tenements and rat-infested slums.

In 1853, sixteen thousand criminals were arrested during the year, one fourth were less than the age of twenty-one and eight hundred were under fifteen. These children had no other way to earn a living and no one to teach them better. Two-

Street Arabs nightly quarters in 1888.

Jacob Riis Collection. Library of Congress.

thirds of New York lived in cramped apartments or tenements. Thousands of children ended up working on the streets of New York in the 1850s, for any number of events could send parents and children reeling in opposite directions. The children were feared and reviled as street rats and guttersnipes, vagrants, beggars, and waifs of the city.

Newsboys were the sons, and occasionally the daughters, of day laborers, piece workers, and traders. Many were the children of immigrants. In the 1850s, New York claimed between five and six hundred newsboys, most of whom came from poor Irish or German families. The adolescent labor force expanded in the 1880s and 1890s when eleven million new immigrants (mainly Jews and Italians) poured into the country. Working-class children entered the adult labor force between the ages of six and fifteen.

The street boys who are pickpockets have their own language so they can recognize one another and converse in a crowd. A watch is a "thimble" and a pocket book a "dummie" in order to "tip a bust." Some keep jobs as bootblacks, peddlers, bill posters, pin boys, canal hands, newsboys, banjo players, birdcage makers, gathers and sellers of driftwood, rag pickers, theater prop managers, sandpaper boys, cattle drivers, and horse holders, and some young girls engaged in prostitution.

Relief and social welfare agencies were unknown, and the city lacked resources for help. New York had the highest death rate of any major city in the world. Thousands of vagrant children roamed the streets of Lower Manhattan seeking food and shelter. They lived by their wits, sleeping in barrels, under steps, and in old boxes. They dined on discarded remnants. The city was unwilling to accept responsibility for them, and most ignored the urchins. Though many children became newsboys, collectively homeless street children were referred to as "newsboys", as it was challenging to differentiate among them. Their suffering and neglect lasted three quarters of a century.

A RETURNED STREET BOY'S SPEECH

The New York Times
January 16, 1875

Credit: The New York Times page 8.
A Returned Street Boy's Speech

Newsboys shooting craps in a jail alley after 10 pm in Albany, New York, 1910.
Lewis Hine Collection. Library of Congress.

The newsboys, at the well known newsboys lodge home in New Chambers Street, were much impressed by the appearance there on a usual Sunday evening meeting, of a well dressed young gentlemen who was introduced as 'a former' street boy from the Fourth Ward, sent to the West by the Children's Aid Society.

After some preliminary remarks by the young gentleman of a general moral nature, which were not appreciated, he said, "Boys, I was just like you once. My father was a longshoreman, and he lived down in a cellar in Roosevelt Street, and I have been there, but I cannot find my people or the house. I use to loaf about the streets, and stole lead from the roofs, and took it to the pawn broker's, and with the money I got a ten cent ticket for the "Old Bowery." It isn't where the Bowery Theatre is now, for that was about eighteen years ago. I made my meals from the ears of corn which people threw away after buying them from an old colored woman who kept a stand in front of the theatre. Sometimes I stole things from the stand. I would turn in for the night in a box, and nearly froze (at this point much hilarity among the boys arose as if at a familiar experience). The fact is I was growing up a thief, and a vagabond, and my parents weren't of much good to me. When my father came home at midnight, drunk, he used to beat me black and blue with the end of his strap, and strike my mother till she foamed at the mouth (at this narrative of domestic experiences there was a sinking of eyes and heads among the boys as though they knew only too much of such scenes). So I took to the streets, and never went home. I should soon have been on Blackwell's Island or at Sing Sing if the Children's Aid people hadn't found me, and sent me West.

"I remember I went out in a party of about thirty, and I was the worst of the whole bunch so that I was the last one taken by the farmers when it came time to choosing us. I went to Indiana, and my employer was a large farmer and a good man. He put me in school during the winter, and he gave me a calf and a pig. I tell you boys, it's fun to sit before a big wood fire at night and toast apples, and hear people talk, and know your calf is growing in the barn, and will soon be a cow which you can sell and make some money. I kept my stock and sold them, and then I turned over the money in one way or another. I studied hard at school, and by and by I taught school myself in the winter, and at last I had three hundred dollars saved. So I told my employer I wanted to go to Yale College, and study for the ministry. He advised me against it, and said he would give me a farm of forty acres if I would stay. I said no, and I went on, and I have worked my way through in one way or another. Sometimes I rang the bell, sometimes I did jobs. This summer I sawed wood for eleven hours a day, and earned something. Now I am studying for the ministry in this City of New York.

"Now boys, my advice to you is not to be content with being on the street always. Try for something else other than being bootblacks and newsboys, and see if you can't make men of yourselves." A storm of applause followed, and a virtuous attitude filled the room. Various sharp little rovers appeared at the office of the Children's Aid Society in Fourth Street the next day to 'go west.'

Newsies amusing themselves while waiting for morning papers in New York City, 1908.

Lewis Hine Collection. Library of Congress.

THE NEWSBOYS LODGING HOMES

Lodging houses once supported by the Children's Aid Society at No. 422 West Twenty-Third Street, New York, New York.

1854 – On June 28, 1854 the New York Times reported the first lodge house for newsboys was located at 128 Fulton Street, New York, New York, on the corners of Fulton and Nassau streets. Fewer than fifty boys occupied the top floor (sixth story) of the New York Sun building when it opened on March 18, 1854. The floor level held all the basic living necessities for the boys at six cents a night. A sign hanging over the white-washed door read, "Newsboys Lodging House." Mr. C.C. Tracy is the Superintendent followed by Mr. C. Weigand and Mr. Charles O'Connor.

1859 – The Girls Lodge House, also known as the Fourth Ward School, at 181 Cherry Street boarded lodgers, provided meals, maintained classrooms, and taught trades with an instance on sewing skills.

1869– The New York Times reports the first Girls Lodge House was a rented building located on Canal Street near

Baxter. After a few years it was removed to No. 125 Bleeker Street. In the winter of 1870, a spacious dwelling was purchased for the girls at No. 27 St. Marks Place.

- Eighteenth Street Lodging House, located at 211 West Eighteenth Street, New York, New York, was attended by Superintendent Gourley.
- The Children's Aid Society retained the Phelps Lodge House at 325 Rivington Street, New York, New York, in conjunction with nineteen day and twelve evening schools accommodating 9,500 students. Henry E. Hawley was superintendent, followed by Mr. Calder.

1870 – The New York Times gives account that the Newsboy's Lodge House at No. 49 and No. 51 Park Place near Broadway was one of the best-known lodge houses and one of the most interesting. Charles O'Connor was the superintendent. A sign hanging over the door read, "Boys who swear and chew tobacco cannot sleep here." Bootblacks, street vendors, newsboys, and juvenile vagrants were regularly welcomed and induced to profit from influence and instruction.

Boys that came to the lodge oftentimes did not know their own names. They were known as Mickety, Round Hearts, Horace Greeley, Wandering Jew, Fat Jack, Pickle Nose, Cranky Jim, Dodge me John, Know Nothing Mike, O'Neill the Great, Professor, and many others, and all spoke with a slang dialect.

The boys arrived steadily at the lodge in the evening around 11:00 pm, while others drifted in around midnight before the doors closed. The latecomers were charged a little extra. By morning breakfast, the boys were gone for the day to assemble their riches selling newspapers poorly clad and barefoot. Requests were regularly made to the public for money, clothing, and donations of most any kind, as most of the boys were poorly protected against the nipping frosty morning air of winter as they went coatless and barefoot to sell papers or black boots.

Two hundred and sixty lodgers paid fifteen cents for supper, bed, and breakfast. The meals consisted of tea, coffee, bread and butter, syrup, and occasionally meat stews and hash. They attended prayer meetings and received instruction with good advice from Lucius Hart, Judge Kirkland, and the boy's good friend Charles L. Brace. Every two weeks some of the youngsters were sent west by the Children's Aid Society bound for trades. Since the first newsboys lodge experiment, 33,000 children had been placed in homes in the West to become farmers and mechanics.

The New York Times
March 27, 1874

Credit: The New York Times page 5. The Latest Work of the Children's Aid Society;
Opening of the New Building for the Newsboy's Lodging House

The Newsboys Lodging Homes

The Brace Memorial News Boys
Lodging House.

The Children's Aid Society Collection.

An innovative Newsboy's Lodge House erected at the intersection of No. 9 Duane, 244 Williams, and 14 New Chambers Streets, also known as the Brace Memorial Lodge House, opened its doors in March of 1874. This lodge took the place of the No. 49 and No. 51 Park Place Lodge House. The building was suited for its designed purpose. The basement and first story was used for business and was a self supporting establishment. The second floor held dining rooms, and the third floor included a school room equipped with moveable desks. This room was also used as a night school for instruction where the boys could learn reading, writing, spelling or listen to brief explanations of history and geography. The fourth and fifth floors held the dormitories with separate beds. The beds were a luxury a newsboy did not encounter, and the lodges Superintendent, Mr. C.C. Tracy, found waking the boys difficult. One newsboy hollered, "Hey! Did ye nivir see a bed afore?" he told Mr. Tracy to, "jest go in airily and tell 'em the steamers in, that will git 'em moving right fast." The sixth floor was turned into a well fitted gymnasium. The main rooms were in all respect suitably furnished and well ventilated with every modern improvement including kitchen accommodations, ample laundry space, and excellent bath rooms. Representing all with health, cleanliness and comfort, this building could accommodate five hundred.

When the newsboy applied for admission into the lodge house he gave his name, age, and occupation. He stated if he could read and write. He then paid six cents and became an independent lodger. For an additional six cents, he was entitled to his supper. He was furnished with a closet with lock and key in which to put his clothes.

A December 25, 1855, New York Times article acknowledged that one lodger, Danny Sullivan, nicknamed 'Professor,' was happy to be back at the Children's Aid Society's lodge after his return from Boston. He had tried to sell books and almanacs, and scarcely cleared his expenses. He had not purchased a license for selling papers, which cost a dollar. He sang in theaters and saloons to gain a few cents, and paid a shilling a night for lodging.

Washing up at the Duane Street Newsboys Lodge House in 1890.

Jacob Riis Collection. Library of Congress.

THE NEWSBOYS LODGING HOMES

1874 – Charles O'Connor began part-time employment with the boys at Fulton and Nassau street according to the New York Times, and progressed to the lodge at Park Place, which he managed for thirty years, watching over 200,000 boys, including one thousand who turned out to be Union soldiers. When lodge conversions took place, O'Connor devoted his full-time efforts at the Duane Street lodge.

The New York Times published an account that Charles O'Connor died on March 12, 1887. Viewing took place at the Newsboy's Lodging House at 14 New Chambers Street. Reverend Cornelius B. Smith of the Church of St. James office acted at the Episcopal service. Among those present were Reverend C. L. Brace, secretary of the society, Charles E. Whitehead, Howard Potter, Judge Van Vorst, William A. Booth, Geo. S. Coe, J. Kennedy Todd, R. Hoe, and R. J. Livingston.

1887 – Rudolph R. Heig, a former newsboy, and employee at the office of the Children's Aid Society, took over as superintendent at the Duane, Williams, and New Chambers Street lodge. Heig rendered his services for twenty-three years until his retirement in the summer of 1910 due to ill health.

1880-90 – The East Side Lodging House, located at 287 East Broadway and Gouverneur Street, took the place of the Phelps Lodge at No. 327 Rivington Street for newsboys and bootblacks according to the New York Times. Mr. George Calder, the superintendent at Rivington, continued his duties at East Side. The lodge house was built by philanthropist Catherine Lorillard Wolfe, and presented to the Children's Aid Society. Moving to the new location meant the boys had to carry their own effects. "Mike," having a bundle larger than he could carry under his arm, was a grade above the rest as he paid another boy six cents to carry his things. Mike also paid a deposit of fifty cents for two keys and two lockers. He paid ten cents for one of the "upper ten" beds, dubbed so because these beds were more accommodating and were separated by venetian blind partitions. The other 175 beds rented out for six cents a night. Once in their new home, 150 boys blissfully examined the dormitories' soft beds.

1884 – The West Side Boy's Lodging House, located at 400 Seventh Avenue and 201 West Thirty- Second Street, New York, New York, opened May 22, 1884, and was gifted to the Children's Aid Society by John Jacob Astor. By 1902 The New York Times reported sale of the property to Samuel Rea of the Pennsylvania Railroad. B.W. Tice is the superintendent.

1887– The Tompkins Square Lodging House, located at 295 East Eighth Street, also known as 127 Avenue B, New York, New York , was a building erected with a gift of $50,000 given to the Children's Aid Society in March by Mrs. R. L. Stuart. [A November 29, 1895, article from the New York Times references Mr. Dupuy as superintendent.]

BRACE TRIBUTE

A commentary by the New York Times on December 9, 1895, described a special tribute at No. 9 Duane Street at the Brace Memorial Lodging House with the unveiling of a tablet incorporating a medallion portrait of the founder, Charles Loring Brace. The six-feet-high tablet and the life-size medallion bust was initially presented to the site by the late Egisto P. Fabbri. The inscription reads, "In Memory of Charles Loring Brace Founder of the Children's Aid Society."

Present for the unveiling were over a hundred newsboys seated left of the hall under the charge of superintendent Heig. The president of the society, D. Willis James, delivered a speech about Brace, in part saying, "He did this all for you and those boys who have preceded you, and whatever they and you are in the future, you will always be grateful to him." Charles E. Whitehead, the vice president added, "If we should read the simple, modest, pleading appeal by which Mr. Brace's life's work in New York was inaugurated bearing the date of March 1853, and turning from that visit twenty-one industrial schools, twelve night schools, seven lodging houses, and the five country charities adorning this city and neighboring shores, we then recognize the fruits of his labor."

In 1850, Charles Loring Brace, philanthropist, missionary, and social worker, made a tour of England, Ireland, Hungary, and parts of France and Germany. He studied the management of schools and prisons and became interested in philanthropic work. In 1852 he set out to minister to the poor at Five Points in cooperation with Mr. Pease and Mrs. Olin, extending his work to the prisons and almshouses of New York City. Through his efforts, the Children's Aid Society was established in 1853; he served as secretary and principal executive officer.

The Society furnished one million meals while sheltering and clothing over 20,000 children. Seventy-five thousand homeless and friendless children had been transplanted from the streets of New York to homes in the far West, and 300,000 had been trained in an industrial school, gaining employment and homes thanks to the efforts of an earnest and persistent Christian. All of the lodging houses grew out of the Newsboy's Lodging House founded by Brace in 1854.

Brace, an editorial writer on The New York Times for over twenty years, wrote and published many books, including Sermons to Newsboys (1861), The New West (1868), and

No. 9 Duane Street Lodging House in Manhattan, New York, opened its doors on March 26, 1874, replacing an earlier lodge house at No. 49 and No. 51 Park Place. The replacement stood on the east side of Williams Street, between Duane and New Chambers streets. Since the lodge stood at the intersection of three streets, the address was also given as 14 New Chambers Street and later 244 Williams Street. The lodging house was near Newspaper Row.

The Children's Aid Society Collection.

The Dangerous Classes of New York and Twenty Years Work Among Them (1880, 3rd edition). A Yale theologian, Brace died at Campfer, Switzerland, August 11, 1890. Brace's sons, Charles Loring Brace (named after his father), James P. Brace, and Robert N. Brace, took over the mission work of the Children's Aid Society.

1887- An industrial school replaced an inadequate Children's Aid Society Lodge House at 709 East Eleventh Street. This four-story brick building located on the corners of Avenue B and Eighth Street overlooked Tompkins Square. The new building was trimmed with terra cotta, and hard wood adorned the finishing. The basement held bathrooms with foot and plunge baths (i.e., showers and bathtubs). A gymnasium and main floor were subdivided into a dining room and classroom. Above the basement, an audience room could provide two rooms for an industrial department, night school, and Sunday evening meeting rooms. The two floors above included dormitories of forty beds. Fifteen small rooms with one bed each were for those who could pay ten cents a night.

Little newsie in St. Louis, Missouri, 1910.
Lewis Hine Collection. Library of Congress.

THE NEWSBOYS LODGING HOMES

Lots were bought on Fortieth Street. A monetary gift was promised for a new building to replace the East Thirty-fifth Street Lodging House. The building on Thirty Fifth housed 520 children per night when there were around 11,820 boys and girls to shelter. The Children's Aid Society's greatest need was for special buildings suitable for many children.

1889 - The New York Times recounted on January 18, 1889, that the Forty-fourth Street Lodging House for Homeless Boys, located at 241, 247, and 249 East Forty-fourth Street and Second Avenue, New York, New York, opened and was funded by Morris Jessup. This lodge replaced the East Thirty-fifth Street Lodge. G.N. Bogardus is the superintendent.

1892 - The Elizabeth Home for Girls, located at 307 East Twelfth Street, New York, New York, was funded by Mary B. Wheeler, Mary B. Ceccarini, and Emily B. Wheeler. This building replaced the Girl's Lodge House on Nos. 21 and 27 St. Marks Place reported the New York Times on December 14, 1892.

1892-96 - Fogg Lodging House, located at 532 West Fifty-third Street, New York, New York, was subsidized by the Elizabeth Perkins Fogg estate in honor of her husband, William H. Fogg, reported the New York Times on January 10, 1891. Mrs. E.S. Hurley is the matron.

1925 - The Kips Bay Home, located at 825 Second Avenue, New York, New York, was established as the Forty-Fourth Street Lodge to provide recreational needs for boys and reduce immoral behavior.

The lodging houses ended in the late 1920s. The industrial schools closed, and children were sent to public schools. The Children's Aid Society became an adoption agency rather than an emigration department.

1943 - The Newsboy's House, located at 244 Williams Street since 1872, was turned over to the Coast Guard. The seven-story structure became a receiving and transfer depot for recruits. The Newsboy's House once had its own recruiting station as 2,890 former boys had enlisted for services since Pearl Harbor, acknowledged the New York Times on January 12, 1943.

Near the World Building, two sleepers from the Newsboy's Lodge House at 14 Chambers Street start with papers in 1908, New York City.

The Lewis Hine Collection. Library of Congress.

HORATIO ALGER (1832-99)

A native of Revere, Massachusetts, and a Harvard graduate who studied under Henry Wadsworth Longfellow, Horatio Alger became a nineteenth-century American author who wrote 135 dime novels. Several of his works were described as rags-to-riches stories, illustrating down-and-out boys achieving the American dream of wealth and success through hard work, courage, determination, and concern for others. Generally this view involved significant simplification, as the novelist's characters typically did not achieve extreme wealth, but rather middle-class-security, stability, and solidity of reputation. The author's subjects were content with a place in society, and the newsboys loved the stories of adventure. As a result, superintendent Charles O'Connor extended an invitation to Alger to speak with the boys at the Newsboy's Lodging House on Williams Street.

Alger was immediately drawn into the work of impoverished young bootblacks, newspaper boys, and peddlers when he arrived at the lodge house. From that moment on he grew to regard the Newsboy's Home as his own, and he spent a great deal of time with the boys. He told the boys stories, listened to their troubles, played games with them, joined in parades, and became an elder companion to them.

Alger found material for his stories among his fellow residents. He wrote about them and he wrote for them. His books showed the triumph of poor boys in the face of great obstacles. A few of his books were: Ragged Dick, Mark the Match Boy, Ben the Luggage Boy, Paul the Peddler, Rough and Ready, Phil the Fiddle, Luck and Pluck, Tattered Tom, Sink or Swim, Tom the Bootblack, and Adrift in New York. Alger never became rich from his prose and gave most of his money to homeless boys. Throughout the years, the boys of the Williams Street Lodge observed Alger's birthday every January 13.

THE NEWSBOYS LODGING HOMES

The New York Times
October 27, 1854 -The Experiment

Credit: The New York Times October 13, 1854.
A Night Among the Newsboys. The Latest Work
of the Children's Aid Society; Opening of the New
Building for the Newsboys Lodging House.

Newsboys assembling papers for the New York Sun.
Photo by Kortz.

In the winter of 1853-54 Charles Loring Brace with a group of gentleman came together to organize the Children's Aid Society in New York City. Fifteen men comprised the first board of trustees who discovered and monitored neglected children to gain their confidence and that of their parents if they had any, leading them toward school entry or working to gain a useful occupation. The organization was geared toward the redemption of the class of the city poor, but more importantly the children, as they observed the boys, and the destitution in the city. There were thousands of homeless children, needy of clothing and money, which went beyond Christian influence. The Children's Aid Society wanted to change the impoverished children into industrious citizens, aiding the outcasts from crime, poverty, and disease which existed in the city. The plan was to provide for their bodies first, then improve their habits and character by giving the homeless newsboys an opportunity for a better life. Expectations were for the boys to have a clean place to sleep, have a meal, attend religious meetings and take in teaching classes.

In a short time, the first rooms were utilized in the Sun buildings sixth story on No. 128 Fulton Street (on the corners of Fulton and Nassau Streets). The building was occupied chiefly by printing offices. At the top of a dingy staircase in need of soap and water, the air was pleasing and a whitewashed door was labeled Newsboys Lodging House. Once the door was opened, spread before the eye were two spacious rooms designed to give off warmth and light to induce the boys to spend evenings there instead of grog holes. From the top story of the Sun building, the rooms appeared over Fulton Street. In one dwelling there was a stove in the corner and the walls were wrapped with bookcases, maps, books, papers and prints. The room was fitted with desks and seats from the dismantled premises of the Public School Society. One end of the platform supported a desk and chairs used by men to encourage the boys upon subjects of morals and manners. On the walls hung encouraging mottos like, "cheer boys cheer, all work and no play makes Jack a dull boy, be content with such things as ye have," and various scriptural placards. The dormitory was furnished with neat wooden berths with warm coverings. Each berth held two good straw beds placed in tiers capable of lodging ninety boys. A wash and bath room with warm water conveniences completed the premises.

The New York Times
October 27, 1854 -
The Experiment

Credit: The New York Times October 13, 1854. A Night Among the Newsboys. The Latest Work of the Children's Aid Society; Opening of the New Building for the Newsboys Lodging House.

Newark's newsboys, 1909.

Lewis Hine Collection. Library of Congress.

Exercising constant supervision of the boys at the lodge was Superintendent C.C. Tracy who was supported by C.L. Brace and friends of the Children's Aid Society. Tracy kept a saving table with nearly one hundred compartments and a registry book for the boys who wanted to save money. Each compartment belonged to one boy as ownership. The drawer was opened once in two months so temptation to spend was removed. Mr. Tracy made deposits for the boys that had a preference at the Sixpenny Bank. The money table savings gave assistance to boys who had no coats, caps or shoes, and were in need of direct assistance.

The lodge's rooms opened early in the evening around 6:00 and closed around 10:00 or 11:00 p.m. as the newsboy's vocation calls them up before dawn. Most are out of the building by 4:00 a.m. The boys arrive at the lodge around 7:00 p.m. and wash, sing, laugh and are happy. They are charged a small fee per night for lodging and meals, but no lad would be turned away. The price for a bed for one night was six cents, and several of the little fellows will apply for berths paying down money a week in advance.

One particular night a boy came into the lodge with a ragged and dirty lad who was a baggage smasher from the wharfs. "Here Mr. Tracy, here's a bummer for you," was the boy's introduction. It was necessary to put the dirty lad through brush and towel before becoming presentable. A time later the 'bummer' made an appearance in new clothing. Mr. Tracy told him he looked so good he hardly recognized him. "Oh yes, I look better now," said the bummer, "and one of these days you'll see me walking up Broadway as fine as any of the quills (clerks)." The boys are taken in from the streets, lodged, clothed if necessary, instructed, made clean in body and improved in mind. They are certain of comfortable quarters in cold nights, and cool in warm nights with first rate accommodations at all times. Scarcely a year before, the warmest places for scores of homeless children was the gratings in the sidewalk over steam engines of the newspaper establishments.

The New York Times
June 30, 1856

The New York Times recounts the Newsboys' Lodge House occupies its old quarters at the top of the Sun building at No. 124 Fulton Street, is flourishing with nearly twenty boys lodging there nightly. In winter when the snow and ice are on the earth and in the air, the lads appear more often, and many sleep on the floor near the stove. Earlier a public plea was announced for donations of bedding and quilts. Mr. Tracy who has charge of the Lodge is in Milwaukee with thirty boys for whom homes have been found on Western farms.

Boys sleeping on a steam grate in the New York Sun office.

Jacob Riis Collection. Museum of the City of New York.

RIGHT:
A church corner sleeping area on
Mulberry Street New York City.
Jabob Riis Collection.

Courtesy Museum of the City of New York.

THE NEWSBOYS LODGING HOMES

The New York Times
May 4, 1854

Credit: The New York Times: Walks Among the New York Poor; Homeless Children

"Don't live no where!" Hardly a day passes that the Children's Aid Society office doesn't hear this. There are men and women in the city who know something what it is like to have no country, to feel shut out forever from the old homestead and native tongue to become strangers in a great new world, yet these are men. To be a child and feel weak and hungry and dependent and to know that in all the city there is not a hovel or hole where he can lie down as in a home, leave the child alone, homeless and friendless in a city full of people. A tall lad of fifteen came into the society's office one morning in weak condition, saying he had no home, and that he had been sleeping in the Essex Market Prison. He had gone to the prison as it was the only place he could call home. He had lost his job at the Sash and Blind business because the company changed hands therefore he was dismissed. For three months he had been looking for work everywhere, but placements had already been taken before his arrival. He had cleaned off snow, held horses, and did small jobs. Before going to the prison, he had slept in boxes at the station house.

A twelve year old boy came in ragged with a visorless cap, and had long uncombed hair hanging over his wasted dirty cheeks. He slept in the caboose at the Erie Depot where he smashed baggage and cleaned walks. "Sometimes I make one and six, and sometimes two shillings a day. I can't read or write," he alleged.

A pretty young girl around fourteen from Roosevelt Street fell among bad associates, and was discovered imprisoned in a house of ill repute. She is now committed to the House of Refuge. The girl had been arrested since she was eleven as a vagrant and common prostitute, living in a home poor cellar on Orange Street. Her parents were drunkards, and threw her to the streets as soon as she could walk. With no love or positive influence she was alone, ungrounded, and foolish. She will now fare better in her new placement while others like her may suffer a lonely death as a vagrant ending in the wards of Penitentiary Hospital.

The 'experiment' met with considerable favor, and the public contributed $5,000 in that first year, and over 100,000 boys were lodgers. The Children's Aid Society was sending out 500 children yearly to work with farmers in the West, and thousands served in the war of rebellion. Often the boys were talked and read to, legitimate games played, and letters from old companions who have gone West are read. Sometimes a returned agent recounts experiences in the far off country that excites the boy's desire to participate in a new home.

The Children's Aid Society sustained a workshop for employment, a German and Italian School, and maintained the Newsboy's Lodging Homes out of necessity for the suffering class. Poor girls under the industrial schools auspice of the Children's Aid Society numbered over four hundred. Services were employed under C.L. Brace, E.P. Smith, E.J. Gerry in the fourth ward, F.W. Bogen among the Germans, C.C. Tracy among the newsboys, and N.A. Hyde in the office.

RIGHT:
"Don't live no where!"
Jacob Riis Collection.
Museum of the City of New York.

DEPRAVITY IN ADOLESCENCE

The New York Times
July 13, 1855

Credit: The New York Times: Incidents Among the Newsboys--An Extempore Speech

The boys in the Newsboys Lodge House on Fulton Street have their own fun occasionally, especially when Mr. Tracy is out. One evening after a boy who goes by the soubriquet of "Fatty" (Martie is his real name), a dull looking fellow with a great deal of humor under the surface, thought he would try his part as a lecturer. Mr. N-, the assistant, was so much amused at the effort that he took notes of it afterwards.

The boy mounted the little platform, seated himself with great dignity, and rapping to make order began, "Boys, I want to speak a word to you. I come some way tonight to get speaking a word to you boys! I love to see you boys, and I have a great interest in you boys. You are very clean, and nice, and comfortable here, boys, and I am glad to see you so. I was a boy once myself. I can never be a boy again. More the pity!" (shaking his head with mock gravity.) "I was once just like youse. I used to pitch pennies, and chew tobaccer, and drink rum, and smoked cigars, just as you do."

Newsies smoking outside a pool hall, St. Louis, 1910.

Lewis Hine Collection. Library of Congress.

110

"I'll swear to that," murmured a boy from the seats. "Yes, boys, I was once a boy myself and I feel for you boys, and I am glad when I have an opportunity to talk to you. Now, how many of you boys made money today?" "I did," said one boy; none of the others spoke. "Only one boy made money!" at this point a noise arose. "Now, boys! boys!" rapping his fist on the table, "I want you to listen attentively, so that I can hear a pin drop. If I cannot hear a pin drop, I cannot speak at all. If you do not wish to hear me, I will stop. There is no use in my coming way up here, and climbing up all these stairs, and leaving my friends at home if you boys won't listen to what I have to say." This restored order in some degree, though some of the lads were near rolling off their seats in convulsions of laughter, for the manner and emphasis of the speaker was even better than his words. "Well, now, how much better it would have been for you other boys to have made money, and not a loafin' about corners and pitchin pennies, and losing your time drinkin. O boys! I used to like rum once. Two thousand and five hundred dollars, all but a cent, were pulled from my pocket in two years by rum. Be men! Quit it. There is another thing I want to speak to you about—that

Newsboys begging tobacco coupons in Philadelphia, 1910.
Lewis Hine Collection. Library of Congress.

is sellin papers on Sunday. It's not right. You knows it isn't. You ought to go to Sunday school—-to Sunday school, boys! After you come out you would (here Fatty was at a loss for virtue) maybe you would find a purse of money!" This was too much; the boys roared out, but he kept his self possession and continued. "Now boys, would it not be better to find a purse of money than to sell papers?

"Boys, take my advice, and stop

selling papers on Sunday. I have a great deal more to say, if you would be quiet. Order! I am sorry you won't listen, but it is bed time and I'm sure you boys are tired." "Yes, yes," said several, "we'll hear you tomorrow night." "Very well boys, I'll be happy to come up tomorrow night and talk to you." The applause was enthusiastic. "We'll have a night at the Tabernacle with Fatty," said one, and another thought he would "beat Sam Houston."

A visitor in the school room overheard Martie very seriously say to some of the boys who were making noise, "Boys, you ought to conduct yourself the best you can when you see a strange gentleman that comes to see you. He'll think more of you newsboys, and put more dimes in your bank if you deserve it. Don't drink rum, and you won't be always a mussin! I don't drink no lager beer, but takes my coffee at the Nassau! I takes my three plates of hot cakes, too, and then I feels in good humor with you all!"

Some of the boys chat agreeably together on the affairs of the day or the doings at Tammany Hall and the Tabernacle, while others are seen stitching the rents of wear and tear that time has made in their pants. When Paddy Moore was asked why he didn't have any buttons in his pants for his suspenders, he simply replied, "sure the holes will do as well Sir."

RIGHT:
The newsboys of New York.
The Children's Aid Society Collection.

"A group of homeless New York street boys. Most of the boys who frequent the lodge homes are waifs never knowing parental care. By regulation they are known by nickname, and speak of each other only by these names. They are proud of their name banner, which often represent some particular oddity or trait."

Darkness and Daylight of New York, Helen Campbell, 1891.

Whitey	Yaller	King of Bums	Bumlets	The Snitcher	Kelly the Rake
	Dutchy	Slobbery Jack	King of Crapshooters	Sheeny	Snoddy

Whitey's blonde hair was nearly white, Dutchy was a German lad, Yaller was of soft brown complexion, Slobbery Jack spills on himself, King of Bums is unsuccessful, King of Crapshooters was fond of tossing pennies and throwing dice, Bumlets was chief speaker, Sheeny was a mystery, The Snitcher tattled a great deal, Snoddy or Snipe Shooter smoked cigar stubs picked out of the gutter, and Kelly the Rake appropriates to his own use anything he can get his hands on.

112

THE LECTURE OF PADDY MOORE

The New York Times
December 22, 1860

Credit: The New York Times supplement section

After Charles Loring Brace made a speech to the newsboys, he challenged the boys to present their own 'talker' and Paddy Moore was unanimously elected. The bright eyed, short nosed small form of a twelve year old stood upon a stool. He began, "Bummers, Snoozers and Citizens! I've come down here among ye to talk to yer a little. Me and my friend Mr. Brace have come to see how yer gittin' along, and to advise yer. You fellers what stands at shops with yer noses over the railin smellin ov the roast beef, and you fellas who's got no home, think of it how we are to encourage ye. I say bummers, for you're all bummers, and so am I. I hate to see ye spendin your money on penny ice creams. Why don't you save your money? You fellers without boots, how would you like a new pair, eh? Well, I hope that you may get 'em, but I rather think you won't. I have hope for you all. I want you to grow to be rich men, citizens, government men, lawyers, generals, and men of influence. Well boys I'll tell you a story. My dad was a hard 'un. One beautiful day he went on a spree, and comes home, and he told me,

A young newsboy in New York City, 1913.

Lewis Hine Collection. Library of Congress.

where's yer mother, and I said I didn't know, and he clipped me over the head with an iron pot, and knocked me down, and me mither dropped in on him, and at it they went. Ah, and at it they went, and at it they kept, ye should have seen 'em, and wilst they were fightin, I slipped me self out the back door and away I went like a scart dog. Well boys I went on till I kim to the Home for the Friendless (this caused a great deal of laughter among the boys who were at that New York City institution) and they took me in, and did for me without a cap to me head, or shoes to me feet, and thin I ran away, and here I am. Now boys (Paddy said with great solemnity), be good,

mind yer manners, copy and see what you'll become." At the conclusion of Paddy's simulated impression of the Superintendent of the lodge, the boys raised a storm of applause. At this junction huge pans of apples were brought in, and the boys soon engaged in the delightful fruit as the matron gave out a hymn while all joined in singing.

The first lodging house on Fulton Street sheltered thousands of waifs plucked out of coal boxes, heaps and places of the street. The success of reclaiming these boys, and diminishing juvenile crime in New York led to establishments in Philadelphia, Chicago, and other large cities with gratifying results.

DISPATCH

The New York Times
March 19, 1869

Credit: The New York Times page 2. The Newsboys Lodging House

The newsboy's lodging house which Mr. Charles O'Connor is Superintendent at No. 49 Park Place is constantly in receipt of letters asking for boys and girls to be sent West. The following was received from Prairieville, Missouri March 2, 1869.

To the Superintendent of the
Newsboy's Lodging House,
No. 49 Park Place, New York, New York.

Dear Sir,

I wish to know if you can send me four good boys from sixteen to eighteen years old. I will board and clothe them. I will give them a good common education, and make first class farmers of them and at the age of twenty-one I will locate them on forty acres of good land, and fix them for farming.

I would also take a girl from sixteen to eighteen years of age, and give her the same home advantages, and the same quantity of land when of age.

Respectfully yours,
Colonel Charles L. Davis

A company of boys left this organization for the West on March 31, 1869.

Bowery gum vendors in
New York City, 1910.
Lewis Hine Collection. Library of Congress.

Newsboy and girl selling papers
around a saloon entrance in the
Bowery of New York City, 1910.
Lewis Hine Collection. Library of Congress.

OUR STREET BOYS IN THE WEST

A Double Mistake Concerning The Character of The Boys Sent, And The Kind Of Homes They Find.

The New York Times
January 19, 1879

Credit: supplement to The New York Times page 10. The Fayette, Mo. Advertiser January 2, 1879

The impression prevails in many localities west of the Mississippi River that the children sent out by the Children's Aid Society, of New York, are the vilest, and most incorrigible among the hoodlums, which infest the highways and byways of this great City. This is a mistake. On the other hand, the impression is current in New York, among those interested, that the people of the West want these children only for profit, which may be derived from their labor in plain parlance, to utilize them as servants. This is also a mistake.

Regarding the former, we have from a reliable authority, Mr. C.L. Brace, that all the children sent West by the society is honest, and worthy. Many of them have enjoyed the comforts of home, the instruction of pious parents, and the advantages of public schools. Others not so fortunate in these respects, have been selected by the society for transportation to the West, only against the most rigid and satisfactory investigations. Naught can be brought against any of them, save their poverty, but it is this that brings them here. As to the notion that these children are brought here, and delivered over

into a species of slavery is ridiculous. They are given only to those persons known to be humane and charitable, and whose condition in life enables them to rear the children properly. Occasionally it may happen that a child finds a hard taskmaster, but not often. Some of the children, who are sent out from here, do not come from better homes than they receive. Generally, it is just the reverse. They are expected to take part in the usual avocations upon the farm with the other children of the farmer, by whom they may happen to be adopted. They often rebel as soon as the novelty wears off, and homesickness for New York begins to tell.

One little fellow, about ten years of age, a remarkably bright child, was sent out last June, and was taken into a most estimable and kind hearted family near this place. He was given several nice suits of clothing, quite a little library, and a gun. He expected to pass his time riding horses, and hunting Indians. Unfortunately, for his peace of mind, he found that there were no Indians here, and instead of riding horses all the time, he was expected to make himself useful by catching them for other purposes. His

A small newsboy asleep on his papers, Jersey City, New Jersey, 1912.
Lewis Hine Collection. Library of Congress.

own parents could not have been kinder to him, or more solicitous as to his welfare than were the parties with whom he lived. Nevertheless, in the course of a few weeks he left. The people of the East who think the children sent are made slaves form their opinions from reports of just the character that this boy gave, opinions that are baseless, and unjust. Many truly needy children have found good homes, and return reports of quite a different character. There are plenty of good homes in Missouri for needy and deserving children, homes where they will enjoy every comfort and advantage that the average Western child enjoys, and give him equal chances in the battle of life.

FALLEN COMRADE

During the 1850s through the early 1900s, untraceable numbers of orphaned and homeless newsboys in cities throughout the United States publicly laid to rest many of their peers. These working-class children feared a burial in a potter's field more than their own demise. A pauper's funeral meant the indigent and underprivileged scratched out a meager existence, incomprehensible to the newsboy. There was a correlation between the grid of one's grave and evoked character, and the newsboys wanted better for each other.

The boys articulated decisive thought in their words and actions. They collected coins from each other to purchase flowers to lay upon a fallen comrade's inexpensive casket. They wrote notes of sympathy and condolence. They planned funerals, acted as pallbearers, supplied hearses, caskets, or suits of clothing, and sometimes managed the ceremony themselves. They converged for the funeral of one of their own, frequently marching through the very streets where they sold papers.

Some of the boys have been together for nine years, in 1909, New Haven, Connecticut.

Lewis Hine Collection. Library of Congress.

The New York Times
May 14, 1912

Credit: The New York Times. Newsboys to Bury a Friend

Thirteen year old Harry Engel, a newsboy, and some of his companions, began the task of collecting $90 to bury their friend, Thomas Verdon, who was known on the East Side from Fourteenth to Forty-second Street as "The Little Philanthropist."

The lad died in Bellevue Hospital a few days ago, and was the principal support of his mother and small brother. Tommy's father was a street cleaner before the strike, and had not obtained employment since the strike had failed. His mother undertook supporting the family by washing, but collapsed and had to give up work. Since then, it was the pennies that Tommy earned that kept a home. Harry Engle, his partner and his friends, are trying to acquire money to bury him.

Fifteen boys went out among Tommy's customers yesterday with printed slips inscribed: Please help Tommy Verdon, the newsboy, who is dead. Anything that will help us bury him will be appreciated. THE NEWSBOYS.

The boys collected only $4.85, but young Engel was not discouraged. An undertaker had promised to bury the boy on Wednesday, and wait for the youngsters to get the money to pay the bill.

The New York Times
August 11, 1904

Credit: The New York Times page 7. Teddy Got His Funeral Togs;
Newsboy Comrades Chipped In $6.50 for Boy Whose Mother Died

Teddy Wendt, one of a colony of newsboys who flock around the gates of the Lackawanna Ferry at the foot of Newark Street in Hoboken, did not put in an appearance yesterday morning. He had been missing since the night before, and his ragged little companions thought it was about time to find out what happened to him.

One person was appointed to go to Teddy's house at 214 Park Avenue, and inquire. He came back only to be quickly surrounded and pelted with questions. "Why," the breathless courier explained, "his mudder's dead, an' he aint got no clos' to go t' de funeral in." "Let's take up a c'lection fer flowers an' clos'," exclaimed one boy as he took off his skull cap and passed it around. The little Arabs dived deep into their ragged pockets, and produced pennies, nickels, and dimes. When the collection was counted, $6.50 was found in that cap.

A committee was appointed to put the money in the hands of the news agent in the depot, and the crowd went along to see that it reached him all right. "Dat's fer funeral togs' for Teddy," the spokesman explained to the agent. "His mudder's dead. An' say, can yer get flowers, too, wid it?" The agent said he guessed so. "Den git 'em, an' put on de card, from da Kids."

The New York Times
May 15, 1905

Credit: The New York Times page 9.
Newsboys to Bury Mate; Save "Dutch" Johnson,
Victim of Pneumonia, from Potter's Field

Frederick Johnson, nineteen years old, lived for many years in the Newsboys Lodging House at 14 New Chambers Street, died of pneumonia at Bellevue Hospital. Saved from a burial in Potters Field, his former newsboys donated to a fund to provide the burial after asking Bellevue authorities to 'hold the body.' Johnson, better known as "Dutch" by the newsboys, was buried in Linden Hill Cemetery, Brooklyn, New York. The Newsboys acted as pallbearers.

Men carry out a small coffin outside a tenement house in Baxter Street, Five Points, 1865.

Library of Congress.

The New York Times
January 7, 1907

Credit: The New York Times page. 2.
Many at Newsboys Funeral; All His Friends
Liked Eddie, Who Helped a Blind Grandmother

Newsy Eddie Cook Dies——

About every newsie in the district found his way to 24 Chapel Street of Borough Hall in Brooklyn for the funeral of thirteen year old Eddie Cook. Left as an orphaned baby, Eddie had been raised by his blind grandmother. In order for Eddie to receive an education, his grandmother established a news stand in the downtown section of Brooklyn on Washington Street. After school hours Eddie helped at the stand. The pair worked hard to support each others welfare. Eddie contracted consumption (tuberculosis) for several months when the disease finally took his life.

A solemn funeral procession of newsboys, and other young

An eight-year-old newsboy from Philadelphia, Pennsylvania, in 1910, was interviewed by photographer Lewis Hine. The boy was just recovering from his second attack of pneumonia and was found selling papers in a rain storm.

Lewis Hine Collection. Library of Congress.

friends, marched behind the coffin taken to Pro-Cathedral in Jay Street. A simple wreath bouquet with the pennies of Eddie's friends lay upon the bier.

The New York Times
March 3, 1908

Credit: Special to The New York Times page 7. Littlest Newsboy Dead

Herbert Smith, the smallest and youngest boy in the Newsboys' Home at 14 New Chambers Street, died at the Willard Parker Hospital yesterday of diphtheria, after an illness of only four days.

All the newsboys, and Superintendent Heig are disconsolate, because only two weeks ago Herbert, who was only eleven, and very bright and honest, had been the means of sending two boys who were years older than himself to the Catholic Protectory for stealing.

The little chap was an orphan, and until three weeks ago had lived with an adopted mother at Richmond Hill, but she abused him, he said, so he ran away to this city, and was at once cared for at the Newsboys Home.

One day he fell in with the two young thieves on Park Row, who tried to induce him to steal. The filchers came to the Home one night, and Herbert pointed them out to Mr. Heig. Their arrest and conviction followed. The newsboys will bury Herbert.

DINNERS

The New York Times
December 25, 1885

*Credit: The New York Times page 5.
How the Newsboys Eat;
They Devour a Christmas Dinner in 18 Minutes*

The newsboys who live at the Newsboy's Lodging House at Duane and New Chambers Street always get a good dinner on Sunday. Ten minutes is the usual time for consuming roast beef, bread and butter, potatoes, and a cup of tea. On Christmas Day in 1885, six hundred newsboys and bootblacks at the 15th Annual Christmas Dinner provided by William M. Fliess took eighteen minutes.

Three hundred little fellows sat down at once on the simple benches on either side of the primitive oil cloth covered tables on which dinner was spread. They stowed away heaps of roast turkey, boiled ham, vegetables, cakes, and pies and apples set before them, washing all down with steamed coffee. In twenty minutes the tables were cleared, and reloaded again with a substantial meal, and three hundred more happy newsies devoured the same.

"Say Cully," shouted one urchin at another who sat opposite him, "which kinder turkey do you like best, black or white meat?" "Stuffin," responded Cully as well as he could with mouth and hands full of food. "How many dinners you had today Blackbird?" asked a bright eyed Caucasian lad to another youth whose ancestry was Nubian. "Two," responded Blackbird, "Say,

Jersey City newsies at a theater, 1912. Lewis Hine Collection.
Library of Congress.

your no good, you aint," resented the white little street Arab, "I've had four, and I'm going uptown to work a Sunday school this evening. Come on, I'll fill you up." The two went off to try the prospective feast at an entertaining Sunday school.

On the third floor of the lodge house is a gymnasium supplied with the usual fittings and open to the boys who chose to practice. When a reporter of The Times asked one vivacious boy if he was going up to the gym the youth replied, "You must be gilly, you must! Do I look like a fellow what's taking in the gym on Christmas night? Well, I guess not. It's only lambs, and fellows what's broke that goes to the gym on such a night as this. No siree. I'm goin up the Bowery, and take in the theater. They've got a daisy bill on, and fellers, they've got a Dutch comedian

who'd make you die laughin. He's better'n Emmet or Gus Williams, he is. Hope to die if I wouldn't rather see him than Sullivan. You hear me, he's a corker!"

The greater part of the newsboys attend a theater, especially on holiday nights. A holiday is considered a failure, or poorly spent if they do not finish the day by a visit to the theater. They save their pennies for days before the coming of a holiday. Of the six hundred who ate Christmas dinner at the lodging house, four to five hundred were at the theaters by night.

Newsboys, bootblacks and other poor boys were given dinners at the lodges at No. 709 East Eleventh Street, No. 218 West Eighteenth Street and No. 314 Thirty-Fifth Street all under the auspices of the Children's Aid Society of New York City.

119

The New York Times
December 26, 1893

Credit: The New York Times page 2.
Joyous Feast of Newsboys

Christmas dinner at a newsboys lodge, New York City.
The Children's Aid Society.

The numbers of street Arabs and waifs attending the usual Christmas Dinner climbed in 1893. One thousand boys, and about one hundred girls had a merry time at the Newsboys Lodging House on Duane Street. Again, they were guests of Mr. William M. Fliess, who for twenty years has made the hearts of the newsboys happy on Christmas in the vicinity of Park Row. By six o'clock a thousand scrambled into the assembly room of the building, where Superintendent Heig and his wife ushered them in, sixteen at a time, as this number filled one table. Soon all fifty tables were over flowing with hungry boys. When the first detachment had eaten, the remaining three hundred were brought into the hall, were seated, and gorged themselves as well. The boys consumed eight hundred pounds of turkey, three hundred pounds of ham, and six barrels of vegetables, two hundred fifty large mince pies, lots of cranberries, and the other essentials making up a good Christmas dinner.

A few days before, the urchins were provided a Thanksgiving dinner by Mrs. William Waldorf Astor. It is custom for her to provide a yearly feast. One thousand attended this holiday on Duane and Chambers Street. The inmates of the Home were notified, and told to invite their friends to the dinner. Word spread that there would be turkey and pie from Broadway to the East River and from Fulton Street to the remotest alley on Cherry Hill. Six hundred pounds of turkey, ten barrels of potatoes, ten barrels of turnips, three hundred loaves of bread, one thousand pies, and enough tea to fill three or four hogsheads [depending on the size, a hogshead could hold anywhere from 63 to 140 gallons] were provided. The feast was served, eaten, and cleared in one and a half hours.

PRESIDENT'S BIRTHDAY DINNER

The New York Times
April 14, 1902

Credit: The New York Times page 6.
A Banquet to Newsboys; Twelve Hundred Urchins
Guests of Randolph Guggenheimer

In April of 1902, 1,200 newsboys were dinner guests of former City Council president Randolph Guggenheimer. The annual event was usually held on George Washington's birthday, but this year it celebrated the birth of Thomas Jefferson. Mr. Guggenheimer explained to his young friends that his time was taken up in arranging for a reception to Prince Henry.

On previous occasions, only the newsboys of Manhattan and the Bronx had been feasted, but this year by unanimous vote, the boys invited their Brooklyn peers. Under the charge of Herbert F. Gunnison of the Brooklyn Eagle, the Brooklyn boys arrived in five chartered trolley cars, and dispensed at different points of the borough. Each boy, much like a political delegate to a national convention, had pinned on his coat a white silk ribbon which bore a portrait of Mr. Guggenheimer and the words, "Brooklyn Newsboys." As the boys stepped off the cars, Mr. Gunnison and his associates provided them with a "yell" on their way over to the banquet. "Uxtra! Uxtra! Uxtra! come let us in, for we are the

Newsies selling papers near the Brooklyn Bridge at 3 am in 1908.

Lewis Hine Collection. Library of Congress.

newsies of old Brooklyn," they chanted.

The newsboys assembled in the library before dinner to listen to a speech by Mr. Guggenheimer, who told them it was Jefferson's birthday. He asked if any of them knew who Thomas Jefferson was. A boy from the Brooklyn delegation jumped to

his feet, but he was too slow. A Manhattanite in the first row was given the floor.

"He was de guy dat kept his peepers shut for twenty years," he shouted. He sat down amid a roomful of laughter. The boy had confused Mr. Jefferson, an actor, with Jefferson the statesman.

Mr. Guggenheimer's address

to the boys acknowledged, "No boys born outside of America have such opportunities given to them. We are the citizens of a country in which all men are created free and equal. This is something of which we are intensely proud, because it means that we are not only equal before the law of the land, but that we are all given equal opportunities for our future life work. It can not be said of any other nation on the face of this earth, that so many of our Presidents, Governors, Senators, our Representatives, or great lawyers, bankers and business men are self made. Thousands of such men have once been poor boys, and risen to wealth and honor through their own hard work and intelligence. Most of the great business men in the city of New York were errand boys earning two and four dollars a week.

"They began at the foot of the ladder and went upward rung by rung. They found many rivals on the ground floor. There is a great crush there, but there is plenty of room at the top." Mr. Guggenheimer added that the Declaration of Independence was the very spirit of American life and liberty, and it was written by the great patriot on whose birthday the boys were honoring.

The philanthropist and com-

Brooklyn Bridge newsie in 1910.
Lewis Hine Collection. Library of Congress.

munity leader went on to say that if his words inspired any one of the boys to acquire good habits of life and conduct, they will rise from their present condition, and take their place among successful men. That would be sufficient reward to Mr. Guggenheimer.

Particular courtesy was given to the Brooklyn boys to dine first. The announcement was met by cries from all parts of the hall. "Dey's hungry kids, dey'll eat it all up. Say Brook's leave some of de feed." The boys, ages four to fifteen, filed downstairs in groups of 250. The Manhattanites evidently didn't believe in

Jefferson's clause that "all men are created equal" for they kept shouting downstairs, "Hurry up Brooky's."

By the end of the evening the boys put away 700 pounds of chicken and turkey, 4 barrels of potatoes, 4 barrels of turnips, 200 gallons of coffee, 500 loaves of bread, 50 quarts of ice cream, and plenty of cake. Guggenheimer extended an invitation to the newsboys for another dinner next year on Washington's birthday, which was met with cheers and whistles by the Manhattan boys and their brothers the 'Uxtras' from Brooklyn.

The New York Times
September 16, 1907

Credit: The New York Times page 9. Many at Funeral of Mr. Guggenheimer

Many at Funeral of Mr. Guggenheimer
Newsboys Send Mourning Delegation to Pay Last Honors to Lifelong Friend

Memorandum in part:

Randolph Guggenheimer, the lawyer and philanthropist, died after a short illness at his summer home at Elberon, New Jersey last Thursday. He was buried yesterday morning at Salem Field, East New York with Masonic rites. The newsboys, whose friend he was for so long, had a delegation in the gallery at Temple Emanu-El in Fifth Avenue at 65th Street, to do what honor they could by being there, and expressing their sorrow. Guggenheimer had made the boys glad so often, that it was easy for them to be sad. His annual dinners furnished many of them the biggest day they ever had.

They came from the Newsboys Home in Duane Street, which Guggenheimer exerted his attention to a large extent. Numerous delegations were represented at Guggenheimer's funeral.

Newsboys at the Evening Journal, Wilmington, Delaware, 1910.

Lewis Hine Collection. Library of Congress.

CHRISTMAS DINNER

The New York Times
December 26, 1909

Credit: The New York Times page 6.
Feast for Newsboys at Lodging House

A newsboy looking at Christmas toys in a shop window.
Bain Collection. Library of Congress.

More than 1,000 newsboys were entertained at Christmas dinner given by Mr. and Mrs. William M. Fleiss at the Newsboys Lodging House at 14 New Chambers Street. After the boys ate their fill, there was enough left over food to feed 500 Bowery Homeless as Superintendent Heig decided he would feed everybody who applied. The father of Mr. Fleiss, gave the first newsboys dinner forty-nine years prior to 1909, and now his son has taken over duties.

Fleiss congratulated the boys on their healthy appetites, and invited them to "go the limit." The dinner consisted of turkey, cranberry sauce, vegetables, mince pies, and plenty of hot coffee. After dinner the boys went to an audience room where the orchestra played. They danced and sang popular songs for the entertainment of their host and visitors.

The homeless from the streets who came to the second dinner displayed hunger by eating ravenously to indicate it was the first real meal many had in weeks, and some ate three dinners. One old man commented that it was the first piece of turkey he had tasted in 15 years.

While the downtown newsies were dining on New Chambers Street their uptown brothers who sell papers in Times Square and upper Broadway, were enjoying a fine feast in the Newsboy's Home at 247 East Forty-fourth Street. The Christmas meal consisted of everything from turkey to ice cream. After the meal, the boys erected a stage in the living room, and gave a variety amateur vaudeville show of quartets, clog dancing, and ragtime. One little boy brought down the house by singing a Mendelssohn song in ragtime.

The Forty-fourth Street Home is also open to messenger boys, and lads engaged in other followings other than selling newspapers. Room rates a day cost ten cents including breakfast and supper, and was under the care of the Children's Aid Society.

Yet another Christmas dinner took place at the Boys West Side Lodging House, also called the Boys Hotel, of the Children's Aid Society at 225 West Thirty-fifth Street, for 150 youngsters. Mr. and Mrs. Douglas Robinson gave a dinner of turkey and other good things. The boys received a package of candy, a new set of underwear, and a new shirt. Also present at the dinner were patrons Miss Lucy Frelinghuysen and F. Delano Weekes. Mrs. Weekes gave the boys new shoes and stockings. After the dinner the boys paraded into the hall of the Boys Hotel for a moving picture exhibition, followed by singing from the Newsboy's Quartet. Superintendent H. Hennefrund was in charge.

NO NEWSBOYS ON THE CARS

The New York Times
April 22, 1894

Credit: The New York Times page 1.
No Newsboys on Cars

The ubiquitous newsboy, and the patron preserving New York City's street cars are going to part company. It will be a sad parting for the newsboy, but the street cars will go bowling gaily along without him. Tomorrow, no newsboy will be allowed on any of the cars, or the lines of First, Second, Third, and the Fourth Avenue Railroad Company's, or the Metropolitan Railway Company. From the East River to the Hudson, and from the Battery to the Harlem, the newsboys are to be relegated to the sidewalks.

This plan has been discussed among the leading surface railroad men of the City for six months or more. It has been kept quiet, and the railroad presidents did not take the newsboys in to their confidence. Officials and employees of the roads had no inkling of what was coming equal to the conductors and drivers, knowing nothing of the matter. Notices will be posted today in the cars of the railroads notifying passengers, conductors, and the newsboys, that the boys will not be permitted to board the cars to sell papers.

The move is one of the most general ever entered into by the New York surface roads. The Metropolitan Railway Street Company is the local name for the Metropolitan Traction Company.

Five-year-old newsboy jumps on and off moving trolley cars nearly every day, risking his life in St. Louis, 1910.

Lewis Hine Collection. Library of Congress.

It owns the Broadway cable road, the Sixth and Seventh Avenue lines, and several cross town routes. It is the largest railroad combination in New York including its roads of First, Second, Third and Fourth Avenues, very little will be left in the way of surface roads for newsboys' activity.

Two occurrences have led the surface roads to this radical step. The first is the large and ever increasing number of accidents to newsboys. The introduction of the fast running cable has greatly increased the number of accidents to the newsboys, and the companies have paid out large sums of money on this account. Every time a newsboy is killed the railroad is liable to pay $5,000 if

contributory negligence is associated.

The second cause of the rule excluding the newsboys from the cars is the great volume of complaints from the patrons of the roads, especially from the cable lines. Feet carelessly become trampled upon, soiled and torn dresses, and ruined patent leather shoes, are only a few reasons declared by means of angry and mournful letters pouring into the railroad offices.

President Herbert H. Vreeland of the Metropolitan Street Railway Company, the leader in the movement against the boys, vocalized his distress. Vreeland's speech explained, "We have taken this step for our own sake, and for the sake of the patrons of our roads. Complaints have been pouring in on us for many months because of the boys. I guess I have received two cartons of letters about the newsboys within the last six months, many from prominent citizens of New York complimenting us, and telling us of the great conveniences and facilities afforded by the roads of our syndicate, but calling our attention to those newsboys. There was no way of regulating the thing, and so the only way was to stop it altogether.

"Newsboys are of all ages, and they are sent out by people who have no sense of responsibility of the danger in which they place the little fellows. These newsboys have given us a wonderful amount of trouble. Almost all the time one or another of them is getting hurt, many seriously, if not killed. You read in the newspapers of the serious accidents, but the public never hears of the hundred and one trifling hurts received by the boys. There was the case of the boy the other day, a little Greek who climbed in the rear of a cable car, paid no attention to the motorman, jumped off the front platform, and fell under a wagon. His folks came to us and wanted $3,000, and we paid it.

"Our patrons have been subjected to a multitude of annoyances through the newsboys. The complaints have been particularly numerous from those who use Broadway cable cars. Early in the evening people might be going to a theatre, possibly a man and woman get on the car, the man

has on a pair of patent leather shoes, the woman has a fine silk dress. In comes a newsboy, and the car is crowded. The boy pushes and shoves through the crowd, and steps on the man's shoes, and soils the silk dress. The cable car suddenly starts with a jerk, and down comes the newsboy's foot on some old gentleman's corn.

I can assure you that it is by no means a pleasant experience for this person to undergo.

"For a long time the syndicate of the Metropolitan Traction Company has not permitted newsboys on any car of its lines in Philadelphia, Trenton, and Newark, Jersey City or down East. I do not know why a similar rule has not prevailed in New York, except that the railroad people here have been waiting for some man with 'sand' to come along, and put the rule in practice. I've got the 'sand' if that's what they've been waiting for. The new rule will not hurt the newsboys, and will provide a

blessing to the patrons of the surface roads in New York. The boys will sell as many papers, but they will sell them to the people before they board the cars."

President Albert J. Elias of the Third Avenue Railroad Company said the rule would be permanently enforced. "Accidents!" said Elias, "have brought surface roads to adopt the rule forbidding newsboys to sell papers on the cars. The boys are being hurt one way or another on the cars all the time, jumping on and jumping off. No one regulates their movements or prevents their injuries."

A March 15, 1902 New York Times article publicized a ten year old newsboy, Louis Rossi, was run over having both legs cut off by an Eighth Avenue trolley car at the corner of Church and Cortlandt Streets. He died March 14, 1902, in the Hudson Street Hospital. Marching of his friends commenced from his house to the Italian church in Baxter Street.

Flipping cars in 1909 Boston, boy hanging onto the stern.

Lewis Hine Collection. Library of Congress.

126

STRIKE FEVER

The New York Times
July 22, 1899

Credit: The New York Times page 4.
The Strike of the Newsboys

"Please don't buy The Evening Journal and the World because the newsboys have striked! I aint a scab!" and similar notices were pinned on the hats and coats of newsboys all over the City, for the strike had spread from the Battery to the Bronx, and across the Brooklyn Bridge. One boy declared, "Das t'ree t'ousand of us, and we'll win sure."

Joseph Pulitzers' World and William Randolph Hearst's Journal offered their papers exclusively for sale. The strike was for the reason the Evening Journal and Evening World would not reduce their price from sixty cents to fifty cents per hundred. The ten cent price hike was due to the war when papers were in great demand, and the newsboys thought it was time it was lowered. The boys bought stacks of papers paying five cents for every ten copies, but then The World and Journal demanded the boys pay six cents for every ten papers. The price hike enraged the newsies.

In Wall Street, after the Exchange opened, a crowd of boys started a parade, but the police broke it up ordering the urchins away as soon as they gathered. A couple hundred boys yelled triumphantly as they paraded

Newsboy hanging on a street car in Delaware, 1910.
Lewis Hine Collection. Library of Congress.

along the Bowery, and destroyed or cleared the stock in trade from the newsstands where the boycotted newspapers were exposed for sale. The Harlem newsboys had worked their way into a Union, and a number of news dealers leading into the Bronx agreed to refuse the 'Extries' or 'Extras.'

"All about de newsboys strike! We sell 'em 'cept World 'n Journal," the boys yelled to pedestrians along Park Row. The few women who sold papers along Park Row and the entrance to the Brooklyn Bridge, were not participating in the strike, whom the strikers left alone portraying the chivalry of the newsboys because they "aint fightin women."

At Fifty-Ninth Street and Ninth Avenue which is one of the distributing points for evening paper wagons a gang of boys

gathered to demonstrate, and pelted a couple of policemen who were placed to protect the delivery carts. Attacks were made on the so called 'scabs' in the proximity of the World and Journal offices.

Kid Blink (who was blind in one eye) alias Mug Magee, one of the leaders of the striking newsboys described their obligation thus: "Aint ten cents worth as much to us as it is to Pulitzer and Hearst who are millionaires? Well, I guess it is. If they can't spare it, how can we?"

The Kid called a meeting of striking boys in Frankfort Street saying, "Fr'ens, Brudders and Feller Citerzens! We is united in a patriotic cause. The time has kim when we mus' eder make a stan,' or be downtrodden by the decypils of avarice and greed'ness. Dey wants it all, and we kims to 'em day saz we must take the papes at der own price or leave 'em. Di saint no time to temporize. Is ye all still wid us in de cause?"

The cheers were agreeable as a crowd of boys marched into Williams Street. Kid Blink was arrested, and taken to Oak Street Station, but was bailed out later leaving him even more ambitious to encourage the cause. Race Track Higgins, Tiny Tim, Crutch Morris and Crazy Arborn battled along with other newsies for the difference of the penny papers. An extra penny for the newspapers was a penny lost to them. Abe Greenhouse, Joe Mulligan, Donato Caroluci, Frank Desso, Cornelius Boyle and Isaac Miller were also arrested, but the strikers never lost their fighting spirit.

"Jack" Sullivan also formed a group, and "Boots" his spokesperson explained, "It's dis a way, we went to de bloke wot sells de papes, and we tells him dat it's got to be two fer a cent or nuthin. The bloke says, wot are yer goin to do about it if yer don't get 'em? Strike, sez I, and Monix. The bloke sez, go ahead and strike, and here we is!" About this time "Mike" steps up, and says, "They tink we're cravens, but we'll show 'em dat we aint. De time is overripe fer action. De cops won't have no time fer us. What is de sense of de meetin', is it strike?" "Sure Mike!" piped a chorus of voices. "Well den de strike is ordered. Der must be no half measures, my men. If you sees any one sellin' de 'Woild or Joinal' swipe de papes, and tear 'em up, throw 'em in de river, any ole ting."

Fifteen year old H.H. Kuehn was arrested for tearing up some papers belonging to another boy at Thirty Fourth Street and Sixth Avenue. At the West Thirtieth Street Station House he refused to give his address. Before the Gerry Society agent arrived, a number of his comrades went to the station with large quantities of fruit and candy for him. When Kuehn was taken to the Gerry Society Headquarters, large numbers of boys followed.

The Jersey City newsboys were notified that newsy had struck a meeting held at the ferry bottom of the Exchange Place,

A crowd waits in front of the New York Journal Building for newspaper war bulletins, Park Row, New York City, *1898*.

Library of Congress.

and they also decided not to sell Journals and Worlds. Wholesale dealers tried to persuade them to abandon their resolution, but the boys were steadfast. The Journals and Worlds could be found at some news stands, but no boy had them for sale.

Harlem, Brooklyn, Staten Island, Newark, and Jersey City newsies joined the strike. In Harlem, the boys sent a committee to see General Master Workman Parsons at his office on East One Hundred and Twenty-Fifth Street, and asked him to be their leader in free advice. Initially, Parsons thought better of the idea, but eventually agreed to counsel the boys.

In Westchester County representing Yonkers, Mount Vernon, New Rochelle and Mamaroneck, parading newsboys were accompanied by a brass band with fife and drum corps. A thousand stood in line at Getty Square while 200,000 citizens greeted the boys who cheered, and hollered the importance of the occasion. The evening of July 24, 1899, the newsies gathered at New Irving Hall on Broome Street where a neighborhood of tenement immigrant families lived. Five thousand newsies filled the hall, and outside streets. Kid Blink made more speeches keeping up encouragement to the boys.

Newsies in Rochester, Troy, and Yonkers New York; New-

Newsies at the side door of the Journal Building near the Brooklyn Bridge, February 12, 1908.

Lewis Hine Collection. Library of Congress.

ark, Trenton and Paterson, New Jersey; Providence, Rhode Island; New Haven, Connecticut; Fall Rivers, Massachusetts; Cincinnati, Ohio; and Lexington, Kentucky joined the strike. Where the papers were once printing 350,000 copies, was reduced to 125,000. The newsies had won! They had shut down circulation throughout New York City, and from Philadelphia to Cincinnati to Boston, and many cities in between.

The strike lasted for two and a half weeks [July 18 to August 2, 1899]. The new higher price for the papers remained, but the companies agreed to buy back all unsold papers at a one hundred percent refund. During the newsboys strike, the boys demonstrated that workers, even children, could successfully fight for rights against powerful employers, and be successful.

The newsboys constitute an important division of an army of homeless children. Within a few years the U.S. government passed laws that protected child workers and set standards for the treatment of our country's children.

THE MESSENGER BOYS

The New York Times
July 25, 1899

Credit: The New York Times page 3.
Newsboys Act and Talk

Messenger boys on strike in New York, 1916.
The Library of Congress.

The strike fever also spread to the telegraph messenger boys, street car employees, and freight handlers on the railroad piers. The telegraph companies threatened were the Postal Telegraph, the Western Union, and the American District Telegraph (ADT.) The ADT boys were not satisfied with their pay as their salaries were fixed at $3.50—$4.00 a week minus fifty cents per week for their uniforms. The messenger's complaint was in the form of wanting a change in work schedule.

Scheduled hours kept by the boys comprised hours of 10am to 5 pm, 9 am to 7pm, and 1 am to 9pm. The hours were satisfactory, but the boys never knew until night what shift they were to be assigned for the next day. They were asking for rotating shifts so they could reserve themselves for daily activities.

The Western Union boys complained that they work fourteen hours on Sunday, and ten hours on weekdays. They want a ten hour Sunday minus the fifty cents per week charged for uniforms. The boys also wanted the "closed pages" abuse stopped. The boys gave the impression they wanted pay for tier errands, regardless if the telegram is delivered to the person's address or not. Presently, they are not paid for messages they were unable to deliver, due to the addressee not home. The boys get ten cents an hour, plus two cents per message delivered.

The Postal Telegraph boys were paid the same rate, but they wanted fifteen cents per hour, and two and half cents per message with the "closed pages" or "dead head" system abolished. The three company offices responded to the messengers' plea saying, "there was not the faintest chance of this happening, as there were a thousand others in reserve for their jobs."

Messengers absorbed in a game of poker in the "den of the terrible nine" (the waiting room for Western Union Messengers) in Hartford, Connecticut.
Lewis Hine Collection. Library of Congress.

THE CLOTHES EXPERIMENT

The New York Times
April 17, 1904

Credit: The New York Times page 7.
Gawk Cassidy, Glass of Broome Street Fashion,
Makes a Feeble Effort at Flirtation, but is Cut
Out by Slats

A philanthropist dropped in on the Newsboy's Home at New Chambers Street one day in 1904, and took note what its inhabitants lacked by way of clothes, that his heart prompted him to supply the deficiency. Without delay, three hundred suits of clothing in various styles and sizes were sent over to the Home. To dispel a fight among the boys Superintendent Heig set a price of one dollar on each suit, and displayed them in this office for examination, trying on, and final selection. The wealthier of the boys were fitted out, and came glorified in their new refinements at one of their weekly Sunday evening meetings. After eyeing each exhibited suit "Gawk" Cassidy was awarded the blue ribbon. "Gawk's" eagle eye sized up the right suit as being distinctive and over powering.

Clothes may make the man, but "States" Nixon is the authority for stating that they unmake the newsboy. "States" got his name title for the fact that he once had a job with the United States Express company. He left that job to sell papers, and prospered enough that when he picked out his suit, he offered two

New York City newsboy, 1896.
Elizabeth Austen Collection. Library of Congress.

dollars to shut off his competition. He picked a summer suit lined in gray material.

"States" went to work selling papers the next day washed, combed, and decked out in his new finery on his usual corner of Duane Street. It was a fine day until "States" realized that things weren't coming his way. Passersby looked at him in astonishment, and some who knew him didn't buy any papers.

It didn't take "States" long to find out the reason why. He saw one of his 'regulars' buy his evening paper from a despicable rival name "Snipe" Buschwit one block away. "Snipe" was a dirty, patched-up; thinly clad lad that

did not measure up to "States" style. "States" knew that "Snipe" had sixty three dollars in Jarmulowsky's Bank, and was heavily invested into going to the theaters. "States" wondered why his radiance repelled buyers, while the disgraceful "Snipe" collected the pennies.

That night "States" mulled thoughts over in his mind arriving at a solution. The next day "States" was at his old corner dirtier than "Snipe," and more ragged then "Leaves" McNulty (Leaves always wore foliage-like attire), and looking sadder than "Angel" Zeller (who could produce tears on a nickel's bet). "States" heart was full of joy as he finished out his day with adequate sales.

The clothes experiment brought an entirely new element into the newsies life—- "de goils." Because the newsies business adheres to the truth, he has never been popular with the Roosevelt Street 'butterflies' to whom flattery was the bread of life. The new clothes were a factor too, as "Gawk" Cassidy was seen walking along Broome Street with "de real rags" as "Slats" Carter had witnessed.

"Slats" known for his skinni-ness, told the sequel to "Gawks" preliminary success. "Slats" thought if given a fair chance he could beat "Gawk" in any game, so he boldly marched along side of "Gawk" and his girl, and soon had the damsel's attention. Realizing he was losing ground, "Gawk" made a desperate effort to recover by rushing "Slats." In doing so, "Gawks" feet worked against him as he pitched head over heels grabbing, and mixing up his "goils" finery as he fell. That was the end of "Gawk," and the beginning of "Slats." Keep-ing quiet about the incident the two boys soon met when taking in a meal at the lodge house. "Gawk" 'accidently' spilled soup on "Slat's" new finery.

Superintendent Heig soon hoped a hatter, and shoe maker would come forward to trim off the suits supplied to the lads. The experiment's effect on the paper selling business, and its attraction for the girls made quite an achievement. The clothes experiment was closely observed.

Messenger boy and bike in New York City, 1896.

Elizabeth Austen Collection. Library of Congress.

132

THE FIGHT

The New York Times
July 20, 1904

Credit: The New York Times page 7.
Thousands See Fight

Newsboys on Frankfort Street near the World Building, New York, 1908.
Lewis Hine Collection. Library of Congress.

Angered by the report that 'Duster' Cook had told the other newsboys along Park Row that 'Wigsy' had swiped two cents from 'Coon' Thompson in a Frankfort Street crap game, 'Wigsy' decided to "get square" as he put it. Although 'Wigsy' is only twelve years old, he prides himself at holding the Ben Franklin championship. He was going to lay for 'Duster' at the foot of the Franklin statue in Printing House Square. "Hey," 'Wigsy' said addressing the milk-shake man, "you'll have to move your wagon in a minute for ders goin to be trouble see, and I don't want you to lose your shakes when it starts." Just then a courier from 'Duster' arrived with the news that 'Duster' and his gang were waiting in the subway valley opposite the old Hall of Records site. Followed by the boys who wanted to see 'Wigsy' fight, they marched up Park Row where he found 'Duster' inside the triangular enclosure made by the subway fence, opposite the bridge entrance.

"Hey," said 'Wigsy' "is dat tru wot yer said about me?" "If it aint true, I wouldn't said it," replied 'Duster.' "Den choose yer second, and git wots' comin ter yer," held 'Wigsy.' "I'm here to fight! Dese fellers'll see dat I git fair play, and I'm wilin ter stand fer any referee wot' you stand fer. 'Lefty' Burns'll suit me," replied 'Duster' taking off his coat. "Lefty's my meat," said 'Wigsy' throwing his hat and coat to one of his companions. "Now see here," said 'Lefty.' "I want youse fellers to understand dat dis fights on the level, and de firs wots fouls'll git a soak of my mitt, understand?" "Alright," chorused the boys as they rubbed their palms together. The seconds were chosen and 'Lefty' ordered everyone outside the subway fence, except the boys who were to act as seconds, and a man who came along with a big camera so he could photograph the fight by rounds.

'Lefty' picked up a tin can, and hanging it with a stick shouted, "dis is the time gong, and when it sounds youse got to quit, and take yer corners fer de next round. When it sounds again, git in da center, and do yer work. If I kin count ten while one of youse is knocked down, dat is a count out, unless yer git on yer feet, and I'll sound de gong, and you'll be counted out." He continued, "Don't let no guys scare yer wid 'cheese it' for yer can each git away from de cops if dey tries to break into the ring. Take yer corners. Time!"

The boys proceeded to punch at each other. "'Wigsy' feints, and lands on 'Dusters' left jaw," said the referee describing the fight. "'Duster' counters in a right upper cut to 'Wigsy's' chin. Two minutes by the City Hall clock ends the first round. Gong! Take yer corners."

The boys backed up, and sat down on pieces of subway timber while their respective seconds proceeded to fan them with folded newspapers. By this time a crowd of several hundred men

133

and women had gathered around leaning on the board fence of the triangle which the boys called 'the ring' watching round two.

Now and then, the crowds cheered 'Wigsy' when he got in a blow on his opponent's face. The referee continued to describe the fight as loud as if he was shouting through a megaphone to people who could not see the fight, and every minute the crowd kept getting bigger and bigger, until there were at least 2,000 spectators.

Laborers on the subway stopped work, as did the men who were unloading papers at the newspaper offices. Motormen and conductors of the Third and Fourth Avenue lines held their cars long enough to get a glimpse of a round.

The fight went on from one thirty until two in the afternoon. The boys were cut and bleeding, and had faced each other into the ninth round when a clergyman climbed over the wooden fence, and jumped between the fighters.

The boys all fled over the fence and the referee after them. As they converged together again walking down Park Row, the fighters asked the referee for his decision.

"Dat was a draw," said 'Lefty.' "You'll have to meet again some other time. But if dat interference didn't come along, I tink I would have awarded the decision to 'Wigsy.' It was a pipe, but where was de cops?" prompted 'Wigsy.'

Another conflict took place in 1905 with a couple of newsboys who had a difference of opinion, and used the newsboys' method of solving matters. On Forty-Second Street, opposite the Knickerbockers Hotel, a crowd watched every feint and blow with lean enjoyment as a couple of newsies went at it for about ten minutes, and when the odds were fairly even a mediator in white spats pushed his way into the circle. "It will be worth your while to stop fighting boys," said the go between.

"Wot's yer price Mister?" asked Ted the one legged newsboy who was timekeeper. "Well boys, I'll give you as much as ten cents a piece," remarked the man. "Not on your life Grandpa," a dozen newsies shouted. "Go it Jim!" and the fight continued.

But the price of peace went up to fifteen cents each. That was too good to resist. The fighters accepted the price, and put on their coats. Soon the crowds thinned out, and the mediator went away satisfied. He had bought an armistice, not peace, for three minutes later the boys went at it again in another corner of Times Square. A policeman came along, and looked on for a moment, then walked in another direction. When both fighters finally became exhausted, their seconds pulled them apart. The boys promised to finish the fight at another time. 'One-eyed Jack' was asked what the cause of the fight was all about. 'Jack' replied, "It's all over a cent."

Newark's small newsboys, 1909. Lewis Hine Collection.
Library of Congress.

LEMONADE SPINNER

The New York Times
June 26, 1905

Credit: The New York Times page 7. He's a Lemonade Spinner

News travels fast of the bridge newsies hearing that one of their own had a new job. When 'Bonsey' Dobbins met 'Sparrow' Kelly at the bridge entrance, he inquired as to the whereabouts of 'Snubsy.' There came a refrain from the other newsboys that, "Snubsy's got a job!" "Got a job?" repeated 'Bonsey.' "Yes!" exclaimed 'Sparrow.' "He's workin over on Broadway for Jim de Greek." "What is he?" asked 'Bonsey.' "A lemonade spinner," said 'Sparrow.' "Dats a new one on me. I heard of lickin postage stamps, but what's a lemonade spinner?" asked 'Bonsey.' "Why, Jim de Greek wot has de fruit stand got a glass tank filled wid lemonade, and 'Snubsy' spins it ter keep de ice and lemons movin, so dat de district messenger kids git a t'irst on 'em watchin it," explained 'Sparrow.' "How much does de Greek pay?" asked 'Bonsey.' "Twenty cents a day and found," said 'Sparrow.' "Found?" questioned 'Bonsey.' "Dat means he kin have all he wants ter drink himself. It's bett'n a vacation 'cause he kin sit on a soap box all day," said 'Sparrow.' "Well, if I ever sees 'Snubsy's' mitt in a lemonade well, I'd never drink another drop of wash as long as I lived," alleged 'Bonsey.' "Sometimes when de Greek's lookin, 'Snubsy' spins de lemons wid a stick," explained 'Sparrow.'

HONEST NEWSBOY

The New York Times
February 11, 1906

Credit: The New York Times page 2. Newsboy Finds Check; Returns it to Bank

Eighteen year old Harry Spencer, a Harlem boy known by the other newsies as 'Dowie' because of his seriousness, and 'always on the level' with the bunch,' dashed up Eighth Avenue one day with a load of afternoon papers, though, sometimes he stopped at 139th Street. As he jumped from a wagon he came upon a wallet lying in a snow bank. He was shocked when he opened the wallet seeing a certified check of $4,000 and about ten dollars in cash. He took the wallet home and showed his mother. The next day, in the classified news section, a description was given of the wallet and its return to No. 80 Leonard Street or to the Hamilton Bank on West 125th Street with no questions asked.

Spencer made it to the bank as the doors opened. He gave a full explanation to the clerk and left the wallet. The clerk wanted to get his name in case the owner would send him a reward, but 'Dowie' declined saying, "this is the honest thing to do."

THE BALL GAME

The New York Times
September 5, 1910

Credit: The New York Times page 5.
Swarm of Newsies Breaks Up the Game

Libeus "Libe" Washburn, Southpaw Richard "Rube" Marquard, and
Mike Donlin of the New York Giants baseball team.
Library of Congress.

Over 20,000 boys attended the annual baseball treat arranged by the Evening Journal for the newsies of greater New York in 1910. One of the biggest crowds who ever rooted, watched the game held at Washington Park in Brooklyn.

The American and National League teams of New York were originally intended to furnish the entertainment, but so many star performers wanted to participate in the game for the lads, that several players from the Brooklyn Club played on both sides.

The game promised an exciting finish as the Giants led 2-0 against the Yankee aggression in the 6th inning. The Giant rooters took full advantage of keeping a steady roar. Rube Marquard pitched four innings for the Yankees until the Giants scored two runs, and then Fisher took up the pitch followed by Quinn who finished the game.

The Yankees sent their first man across the rubber, and the tide changed. One run was scored, and the Yankee rooters were aroused. In the next inning their favorite team sent in three more runs, making the score 4-2 in favor of the Yankees. Hal Chase was the baseball fan's pride, and played first and second bases to the boys' delight. Chase got the ball rolling for the Yankees when he got the first hit off Hendricks and reached first base. Hendricks did the pitching for the Giants for three innings, then retired to make room for Thompson, who threw until Crabble was sent to the box in the seventh. The newsboys became so restless that it was expedient to cut the game short in the seventh inning as the crowd got behind the police and swarmed the field, running in every direction.

OLYMPIC CHAMPION BABE MCDONALD

The New York Times
November 12, 1926

Credit: The New York Times purchased article page 23.
Newsboys Are Happy; Pat McDonald, Promoted
to Lieutenant

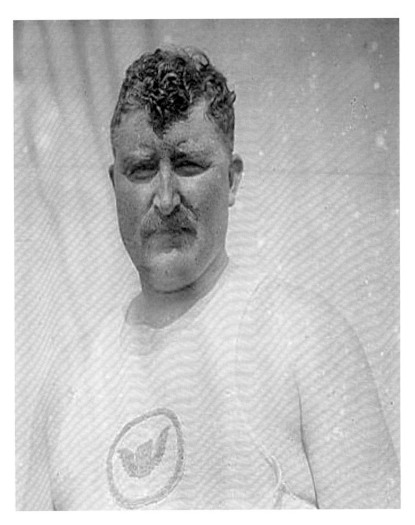

Patrick "Babe" McDonald, circa 1912.
Library of Congress.

"Pat's been made a Lieuten-ant," shouted one newsboy to another in Times Square. The as-sertion meant something only the newsies could acquaint to in the district square. Patrick (Babe) McDonald, Olympic Champion for many years, directed traffic as a policeman at Forty Third and Broadway. The policeman, a giant in stature, was always friendly to the boys, and helped them out of trouble on many occasions. The boys appreciated his kindness so much, that on June 11, 1912 when McDonald was about to sail to take part in the Olympic games, the boys presented him with a loving cup. "I am very proAud," said McDon-ald when he received the cup. "Thanks boys. I cAonsider this a great honor, and to show my appreciation, I will try my best to bring back ten points for the American team."

Babe did well in those games, and when he retuned to his post in New York, he again re-ceived a welcome from his young friends. In December of 1920, McDonald was promoted to Ser-geant, and in 1926 he advanced to Lieutenant. Babe's ability as a weight thrower was well known, but he also was a great swim-mer, and on occasion saved many persons from drowning.

McDonald was a New York policeman from 1905 to his retirement in 1946. For many years he took the outdoor and indoor shot put championships. He won gold medals in the shot put at the 1912 Olympics, and the fifty-six pound weight throw at the 1920 Olympics when he was forty-two. His promise to the newsboys to bring home the gold was genuine.

NEWSBOYS DEBATE ON WOMEN'S SUFFRAGE

The New York Times
December 21, 1910

Credit: The New York Times page 8.
The Newsboy View of Women Suffrage

The newsboys of the West Side Boys Lodging House on Thirty Fifth Street debated Women's Suffrage with the newsboys of the Chambers Street Lodging House. The West Side boys had the choice of which side of the argument they would take. They chose the affirmative side that women should have the right to vote. The Chambers Street boys went about to public libraries researching the anti-suffrage argument.

The debate was a maiden effort of the Newsboys Literary and Debating Society organized by James E. Sandefur, a good natured young lawyer. Sandefur only had two short weeks to train the Chambers Street boys before the debate. The West Side boys had been debating topics for two years which was evident when their first speaker, sixteen year old Richard Palmer, opened the affirmative side.

"Honorable judges, ladies, gentlemen, and fellow newsboys," he began gripping the cast iron railing of the platform addressing a crowd of two hundred. "Shall women vote will be discussed from three points. Is it right? Is it expedient? Is it practical? Until the days of the American Revolution there was only one form

Suffrage demonstration at Park Row in New York City, 1913.
Library of Congress.

of government, and that was a monarchy. After the Declaration of Independence, all men were given equal rights, and that means women too. In monarchial days, women were not taxpayers and wage earners, or actively engaged in building up the country as they are today."

Ave Levy, a postal messenger, speaking first for the Chambers Street newsboys on the negative side began, "If we give the vote to women because they pay taxes, we will have to give it to foreigners who also pay taxes. Giving women the ballot has been unsuccessful in all the states in which it has been tried. In Colorado there is just as much drinking by women as men." Martin Landes for the West Side

interjected, "and they're not very chivalrous either!" "Spell it! Spell it!" shouted the other newsboys.

Eighteen year old Malcolm McDougall, a Scotch boy, spoke next for the negative side. "The reason women should not be given the ballot is because she can't back the laws up after she passes them. The ballot she casts may make a war, but when men go out and fight, she'll have to stay at home. Suppose a man was going to be hanged for murder, and he refused to be hanged, what could women police do about it?"

James Rattigan interceded for the West Side about the reform institutions across the states. Small Abe Kirschbaum had only three days to prepare for the debate. He was one of the

Chambers Street Team substitutes.

"My dear audience," Abe spoke in a forceful voice. "Women can't undergo the hardships of a war. She can be a nurse. A cat has only nine lives, and like a cat, Women's Suffrage is being killed in Switzerland, France, and all the States into which it has been introduced here. Speaking plainly, and if the ladies present will excuse me, the existing conditions in the equal suffrage states is something fierce. In Colorado there are State Homes for criminal boys, but no homes for honest square boys who are homeless and destitute. The polygamy that is going on in Utah... well it's just something fierce!"

"The Sky Is Now Her Limit," by Bushnell. Labeled rungs of a ladder depict "Slavery," "House Drudgery," and "Shop Work." Top rungs characterize "Equal Suffrage," "Wage Equity," and "Presidency."

Library of Congress.

MEMORANDUM

Early victories were had in 1869 Wyoming and 1870 Utah. The push to grant the vote to Utah women disenfranchised by the U.S. Congress in 1887, was fueled by outsiders' belief that Utah women would put an end to polygamy.

Universally, women's suffrage did not come until the Nineteenth Amendment to the U. S. Constitution was ratified on August 26, 1920. The efforts of both parties led to the passage of the Anthony Amendment which states, "the rights of citizens to vote shall not be denied or abridged by the United States, or by any State on account of sex." Women had finally won the right to vote!

COMPLAINTS OF THOSE NEWSBOYS

The New York Times
May 27, 1911

Credit: The New York Times page 13. Shall Newsboys Holler?

Cornelius S. Loder of No. 30 Church Street asked Mayor Gaynor to do something about stopping the shouting of newsboys in the streets, and sent him another letter yesterday.

> *Hon. William J. Gaynor*
> *Mayor of the City of New York, New York*
>
> *Dear Mayor Gaynor,*
>   *I am interested in the boys, especially those who are obliged to earn a living, and for nearly twenty years I have tried, outside of business hours, to help our younger brothers. I mention this so that you will not misunderstand my writing you in regard to the newsboys.*
>
>   *Your interest in them is known. I approve of their being controlled, and thus helped through a license. But why permit them to yell their wares under office windows, and in certain places? If some holler, all must holler. The strongest lunged out sells the modest little chap, who is entitled to our special consideration. It is often the case of the 'survival of the fittest.' Why should any shout who maintain stationary stands, particularly when we are endeavoring to suppress all unnecessary noises?*
>
>   *Some of the newsboys express problems in trying to rightly guide the destinies of our city, and this is a small matter to bring to the attention of a busy man, but the father of the great metropolis is the regular, and natural channel, which these things must be sifted.*
>
>   *Please permit me to express the hope that you will be able to carry to a successful close everything that is good and right, and in these endeavors you will always have my warmest sympathy.*
>
>   *Respectfully yours,*
>   *Cornelius S. Loder*

   The Mayor informed Mr. Loder that he, "does not consider it his function to interfere with the newsboys."

Newsie selling papers in the
street in New York City, 1912.
Lewis Hine Collection.
Courtesy George Eastman House.

SELECTIONS FROM THE CHILDREN'S AID SOCIETY ANNUAL REPORTS

The New York Times
March 22, 1854

Credit: The New York Times page 5. New York City the Trades

The first four days of the original Newsboy's Lodging House at No. 128 Fulton Street's inauguration acquired 30 boys and 30 full beds. Boys pay 6 cents for lodging, and extra for meals. Advertised announcements placed by the Superintendent at No. 128 Fulton Street:

- March 24, 1854- I received yesterday, 22nd inst., from a lady friend for the newsboys' rooms six blanket pairs, seven sheet pairs, all excellent. In this case it was more blessed to give than to receive, the lady must be happy. C.C. TRACY, Superintendent.

- March 29, 1854— I received two packages of books, and pamphlets today, left in the Sun Office by some kind hand for the Newsboys Lodging House. They were well selected, and just the books to interest, and benefit this class of boys. We need a few slates, and maps. We also need a few volunteer teachers to aid in instructing the boys evenings. Who speaks first? C.C. TRACY, Superintendent.

- May 9, 1854— Dear Sir: Enclosed we hand you a catalogue of our goods. If you find any articles there that will be useful in furthering the objects of your commendable Newsboys Home, we shall take pleasure in contributing such goods as you may find suitable, to the extent of ten dollars. Yours truly, S.W. SMITH & BROTHER.

- May 12, 1854— Mr. Tracy's reply to S.W. Smith & Brother—- Dear Sir: Here is another evidence that business men do sometimes stop and think of others, even the newsboys. The following note and goods were duly received, and I esteem it a pleasant duty to acknowledge it. The note speaks for itself better than anything I can say. Yours sincerely, C.C. TRACY, Superintendent.

Early morning in Donovan Lane
near the Five Points in 1872.

Library of Congress.

SELECTIONS FROM THE CHILDREN'S AID SOCIETY ANNUAL REPORTS

Italian and German Schools – 1855

The Italian poor were once packed into buildings situated in the Five Point's filthy, loathsome surroundings. Five Points was centered on the intersection of Anthony (now Worth), Orange (now Baxter), Mulberry, Cross (now Mosco St. /Park Row), and Little Water (now gone.) C.L. Brace circled through the streets, often observing detrimental activities and destruction of mind and soul.

He hypothesized that education would liberate the poor from evil occupations that surround their living conditions and from bad habits, reforming them to prosperity. One result was the Italian School, founded in 1855. The Children's Aid Society's Italian School at No. 44 Franklin Street was well organized according to an 1871 report, and attended by 215 children on average, with a roll call numbering 562. Among the teachers were Mr. A.E. Cerqua, Mrs. Alleyne, Miss Richards, and Mr. Demartini.

In 1875, the new school was sixty by eighty feet, four stories high, and constructed at No. 156 Leonard Street. The Department of Public Instruction in Italy periodically aided with the Italian classes. By 1910, the Italian Evening School was located at No. 155 Worth Street. The boys learned power machinery and factory work; the girls were trained to be efficient housewives. All were expected to master the English language.

Benefitting another ethnic group was the German Industrial School which provided educational and industrial training. Student attendance in 1871 averaged 375, with a roll call of 872. Listed teachers were Miss E. Robertson, Miss A.E. Chandler, Miss A. Strathern, Miss E.S. Lowe, Miss M. Staats, and Mrs. E. Pieligaard. By 1875, the German school was located at No. 272 Second Street.

New York Times
December 21, 1857

Credit: The New York Times page. 4. News of the Day

A company of thirty composed children from the Children's Aid Society, and of the Sewing Girl's Branch Office left New York City in the afternoon under the care of agent, Mr. C.C. Tracy for the west. Dressmakers, seamstresses of all work, factory girls, pen makers, and parasol workers composed the motley avocations of the industrious young women who have availed themselves of the opportunity to better their condition in the land of the west. The young women were neat and modest of appearance, and looked perfectly happy at the fortunate epoch of their lives which had arrived at a time when they had suffered much from the want of employment during the late crisis. The girls had all known comparative comfort until then, and sufficient respectability was proved by the excellent references received at the Branch Office.

The New York Times
February 25, 1858

Credit: The New York Times page 5. Children's Aid Society-the Work of the Year.

Concerning the work of carrying our children into the West, Mr. C.C. Tracy states, "since March 1, 1857, I have taken to the West nine companies." They are as follows:

Date of Leaving New York	Number in Each Company	Where Delivered
March 31, 1857	56	Battle Creek & Olivet, Michigan
May 21, 1857	30	Kal., Battle Creek & Albion, Michigan
June 30, 1857	31	Albion & Marengo, Michigan
August 6, 1857	24	Ypsilanti & Grass Lake, Michigan
October 8, 1857	26	Michigan City & LaPorte, Indiana
November 17, 1857	58	LaPorte & New Carlisle, Indiana
November 30, 1857	34	Jonesville, Michigan
December 21, 1857	30	Cold Water, Mich. & South Bend, Ind.
January 26, 1858	59	Fort Wayne, Indiana
Total: 348		

Regarding the work of aiding girls to the West, Mr. Barlow reports the number of applications received and recorded as 455, the number of girls sent West was 210, and transportation costs total $3,600.00. Many of the girls are not willing to apply for assistance as they dread the publicity. Satisfactory reports are received from our correspondents in the West both from the families, and from our placements, as many write to tell their brothers and sisters to come west.

There are now six Industrial Schools with 958 pupils. An Italian School held at the Five Points House of Industry reports 200 boys and girls attend the school; nearly all comprised of Italian children in the neighborhood of Five Points.

The Newsboys Lodge House this past year is attended by 800 boys, about 50 to 60 each night. The three area boys meetings have been attended weekly by 600. The Girls Lodge House on 181 Cherry Street boards 114, and has furnished 3,588 meals. Around 13,000 garments have been donated to the children from the country.

The New York Times
March 5, 1859

Credit: The New York Times page 2. Homeless Children

The Children's Aid Society's aim is to improve upon a decrease of crime amongst our youth:

1856	Committed to City Prison	1857
282	Girls under 18	70
275	Vagrant girls under 16	57
1427	Girls committed age 16-20	1187
194	Petty larceny	93
639	Vagrant girls age 16-20	550

Cultural disruption developed due to the influx of immigration into the U.S. resulting in poor health, lack of money, and dreadful living conditions. Many children were Irish, or in the later nineteenth century Italian or Jewish. While most of the foster families were Protestant, Brace never doubted his system for effectiveness, as his belief was in rescuing needy children while protecting New York City from "the dangerous classes."

Italian School photo courtesy of the Children's Aid Society Collection.

SELECTIONS FROM THE CHILDREN'S AID SOCIETY ANNUAL REPORTS

This past year 750 children have been provided with comfortable new homes under the guidance of the Children's Aid agent C. C. Tracy. A few thousand have been relocated to the wide West in past years. The spontaneous kind hearts extended to the children from families in the West makes it seem strange that the homeless children of New York City have been so long delayed. Outcast children have been attended through the many Industrial Schools managed by the Children's Aid Society for the poor who cannot attend public schools. The children are fed, clothed, and attend classes. Cost is $15.00 annually, as many benevolent benefactors have contributed to our schools. Besides classes, trades are taught and learned. Girls can learn tailoring and dress making. Evening schools and Sunday prayer meetings aid toward saving influences. 3,000 have been lodged this year.

The Lodge House for the newsboys is not restricted to newsboys. Match sellers, apple vendors, button peddlers, and all who are engaged in petty pursuits are accepted. Most who are regular lodgers, would other wise sleep in market houses, hay barges, old cellars, ash barrels, coal boxes or walk the streets at night, and lounge in drinking saloons by day, or else pile in a heap at night—one boy keeping the other warm.

The New York Times
March 1, 1860

Credit: The New York Times page 8. Children's Aid Society; the Seventh Annual Report of the Secretary

The Seventh Annual Report of the Children's Aid Society records Trustees for the coming year are John L. Mason, James R. Spalding (replaced Archibald Russell), Robert J. Livingston, Wm. L. King, and Charles L. Brace. Directors are President John L. Mason, and Secretary J. E. Williams.

In regard to the Industrial Schools, scholars Miss Gordon and Miss Dunn at the Fourth Ward School at No. 181 Cherry Street, have registered 234 children in the midst of 115 names on roll call. The average student attendance is 92, monitored students confirm 14 have gone to service, 10 are working a trade, 14 have gone to school at the Sisters of Mercy, 10 have gone to a public school, and one has died. 500 garments and 106 pairs of shoes have been distributed to all in need. No meals are distributed to the children other than the staple of bread.

The Hudson River School taught by Mrs. Tracy located on the corner of Twenty Fifth Street and Ninth Avenue, requests a suitable place to bathe the children, and teach them washing and ironing. One hundred six children are registered with 75 averaging attendance. Twelve teacher's volunteer services and the pupils have completed 358 garments.

The East River School near Third Avenue is administered by Miss Spratt. The whole number of students at this school stands at 310, averaging a daily attendance of 112. Thirty teachers volunteer services, bread is the only staple given to the children, and annual expense amounts exceed $750.

The School of the House of Industry at No. 100 West Sixteenth Street, under scholar Miss Patten, comprises 62 students with 50 averaging attendance. The sewing school has 82 pupils, with a complete number of 150. The school has made 130 garments reaching annual expenses of $635.

The Hamersley Street School under the direction of teacher Miss M. Laing retains 56 students, averaging an attendance of 40, and two volunteer teachers. Forty -seven garments were distributed in six weeks, one meal a day is distributed, and expenses reached $500. The Boys Meeting held at No. 23 Hamersley Street under Mrs. Woolsey reports fifty and one hundred fifty attend on Sundays.

SELECTIONS FROM THE
CHILDREN'S AID SOCIETY ANNUAL REPORTS

1860

The Industrial School for German Girls at No. 429 Grand Street has been liberally responded to by wealthy German citizens. About sixty German working girls between the ages of fourteen and sixteen are in regular evening attendance. The usual branches that are taught on week days, set Saturday evenings aside for games and social amusement, meals are not provided, with the exception of Saturday evenings.

This year, homes have been provided for 617 boys, 164 girls, 24 women, and 9 men equating to 814 persons placed out. Receiving states and numbers include:

Massachusetts 4; Connecticut 24; Rhode Island 1; New York 49; Long Island 16; New Jersey 22; Pennsylvania 4; Virginia 7, Ohio 33, Illinois 9, Michigan 10; Iowa 8; Indiana 352; Wisconsin 3; Kansas 3; Missouri 6; Texas 5; Minnesota 1; City 227; Institutions 24; Other Places 6. The Nativity of these individuals is recorded as American 456, Irish 177, German 95, English 14, Scotch 7, French 3, Colored 3, and Unknown 59.

The whole number sent West by the society during 1858 stands at 5,074. Average individual cost per person amounts to $12.00 up from the previous year's $10.00. It is presumed that preparatory steps have been taken toward these children for the rough and tumble of life, and not to be looked upon as a domestic Cooley-trade. Self respect is awakened in them as they do right and tell the truth. They can grow in usefulness and honor with a family in the West, in opposition to the squalors of their current situations. The excellent results of this system are proven in statements made by the families in the West. Ninety out of every one hundred children reclaimed by the society have turned out well.

Boston newsies picking up papers at the Daily Globe in 1909.

Lewis Hine Collection. Library of Congress.

Shoe Shine Boy by J. G. Brown
Library of Congress.

The New York Times
January 29, 1863

Credit: The New York Times page 3. General City News

OFF FOR THE WEST—- A company of 30 children left the office of the Children's Aid Society on Tuesday afternoon under the care of Mr. C.C. Tracy. The children were, as usual, comfortably dressed, and went rejoicing in the change that awaited them in the far West, where all of them will be provided with good Christian homes among the farmers.

February 24, 1863

Credit: The New York Times page 2. The Children's Aid Society; Tenth Annual Report of the Treasurer

The Tenth Annual Report of the Children's Aid Society reports the majority of newsboys and lost lads, who have been saved from vagrancy and a life of crime, add up to 395. All have been turned out to friends and relatives. In the past ten years 7,553 children have been sent West. Of those emigrating, 168 have been newsboys who have volunteered to join the Army. Over 500 are presently serving their country in the Army from the Western homes in which they were placed.

An account is given of the newsboys savings bank at the lodge representing 347 boys who have saved $1,315.16. All boys pay for their supper, lodging, and fines, reaching $1,102.33. The funds have been applied toward the support of the Newsboys Lodge.

The Girl's Lodging House established May 1, 1862, currently lodges 597. Ninety-eight have been sent to situations (work,) and eighteen to other institutions. There are 40,000 children in New York City that never attend a school. Aggregate amounts paid by the Society in ten years arrived at $139,720.98, and receipt amounts calculated toward $143,953.

This boy is selling papers in Washington, D.C. in 1921.
His hat reads: Have You Read The News? One Cent.

Library of Congress.

SELECTIONS FROM THE
CHILDREN'S AID SOCIETY ANNUAL REPORTS

The New York Times
November 25, 1869

Credit: The New York Times page 3. Children's Aid Society; Work of the Last Nine Months

The officers and trustees chosen for the ensuing year are B.J. Howland, Howard Potter, Horatio Allen, Theodore Roosevelt, and Alexander Van Rensselaer. William A. Booth will serve as President, John E. Williams in the function of Treasurer and Charles L. Brace as Secretary. Expenditures for the last nine months (February 1st – November 1st) total $96,978.59 in addition to receipt totals of $94,914.19. Resources have improved through the generous donations from C.H. Shipman and Chauncey Rose. A portion of the Society's funding is granted under the Excise Law, future provisions will be determined through the nature of this law in the Supreme Court.

There are now 19 Industrial Evening Schools bearing 6,813 names with 2,747 students attending. The Newsboys Lodge under the guidance of Charles O'Connor and his wife have furnished 39,077 lodgings and 38,207 meals to 7,383 boys. The boys are charged 6 cents each for breakfast, supper, and lodging, which attains an ambiance of independence. The average number of lodgers equal 160 per night, while accommodations are sufficient for 260. 649 boys have been provided homes, and 642 truants have been restored to their friends. During the past nine months homes in the West have been found for 1,140 boys, 547 girls, 126 men and 117 women.

Besides the Newsboys Lodging House, the Girls Lodging House at No. 125 Bleeker Street accommodates 958 regular lodgers, and funded lodgings for over 10,000 during the past year. The Eighteenth Street Lodge House has furnished 15,506 with lodging, and 15,429 meals. The Phelps Lodging House at No. 325 Rivington Street has provided 16,512 lodgings, and 9,888 meals. The Eleventh Ward Lodging House at No. 709 East Eleventh Street lodges 10,460, and has served 10,589 meals. Most of these establishments have night, day, and industrial schools that charge a trifling rate.

The New York Times
November 30, 1870

Credit: The New York Times page 2. Children's Aid Society; Children Sent West and South

The Children's Aid Society has labored the past eighteen years to prevent the growth of the dangerous classes. Schools that were opened to adapt to the unfortunate are called Industrial Schools. For the utterly homeless, Lodge Houses were prepared, subsequently these rejected little ones are sent away in large numbers to carefully chosen families in the country where they have grown up, and had the best advantages of our best rural districts. In the past year, 2,500 children have been sent to homes in the West, or neighboring districts of New York, most of who would have grown up here to be criminals or burdens on society.

A teacher of an Industrial School near "Dutch Hill" maintains 2,000 pupils of the most degraded under her charge; she reports that only five have become criminals. Vagrancy is usually charged against the girls where they often end up in City prison, but since the Children's Aid Society's work, the numbers have dropped according to police reports. In 1857 there were 3,449 vagrants, in 1859 - 5,776, in

1864 - 1,342, and in 1870 - 871. If the girls were to each retain imprisonment on Blackwell's Island, their maintenance would cost the City $250,000. The girls have been brought up under our best moral and educational influences, showing definite results by a figure of 25,000.

Five lodge homes for homeless children have been sustained providing 150,176 meals, and lodging 136,686. Nineteen Day Industrial Schools have been sustained, and eight Evening Schools, involving 7,098 students with an average attendance of 2,846 pupils. There are five supported reading rooms.

The New York Times
November 28, 1871

Credit: The New York Times page 2. A Noble Work. Annual Work of the Children's Aid Society

Since 1854, the Children's Aid Society has provided homes for 25,216. The following 1871 schedule illustrates the number of children sent to each state, month, and nationality and parentage.

Where Sent:

New York - 447	Michigan - 74	Returned to Friends - 103
New Jersey - 166	Iowa - 369	Other Institutions - 9
Connecticut - 60	Wisconsin - 61	Total - 3,386
Massachusetts - 60	Minnesota - 43	Parentage:
Pennsylvania - 102	Kansas - 208	Parents Living - 927
Vermont - 24	Missouri - 424	Father Living - 65
New Hampshire - 19	Maryland - 3	Mother Living - 191
Ohio - 307	Rhode Island - 26	Orphans - 1,231
Indiana - 34	Nebraska - 68	Unknown– 329
Illinois - 346	City - 432	Men Placed - 303
		Women Placed - 340

Nationality	Month	Number Sent
American born - 1,124	November 1870	292
Irish - 1,058	December 1870	539
English - 199	January 1871	221
German - 375	February	226
Swedes - 127	March	379
French - 19	April	274
Scotch - 56	May	411
Canadian - 10	June	238
Italian - 3	July	196
Austrian - 1	August	391
Unknown - 414	September	335
Total —— 3,386	October	194

SELECTIONS FROM THE
CHILDREN'S AID SOCIETY ANNUAL REPORTS

Agent J.P. Brace traveled 29,748 miles this year, and placed 952 persons. Agent E. Trott traveled 18,310 miles this year, and placed 742 persons. No accidents r difficulties reported, concerning hundreds of the little emigrants.

- The work summary of the Children's Aid Society for the year includes 157,729 meals furnished at the lodge houses, 131,578 lodgings furnished, and 11,928 individuals registered. There were 4,958 orphans at the lodge houses, and the Society sent 1,231 orphans West.

- At the industrial schools, 9,429 persons registered. Sixteen Industrial Schools serve gratuitous meals, and three serve none. The total number of salaried teachers including evening schools arrive at 71, with an additional 51 volunteer teachers. 530 children have been sent to public school. The sum total of children under the charge of the Children's Aid this year reached 24,743.

A forge class of the Children's Aid Society in New York City, 1911 .

Library of Congress.

1871

Mr. Brace says: "We have had the curiosity this year to make a careful survey in each lodging house of the causes of homelessness in a hundred cases from each institution. Among 400 street children taken at random, we find the causes of their condition to be as follows:

Orphans	124	Parent in hospital	7
Intemperance of parents (Alcoholics)	65	Mothers too poor to keep a home	25
Maltreatment by step father or mother	42	Parent in Prison	11
Mothers who live out	45	Mothers deserted them	7
Fathers are loafers	35	Mother insane in an asylum	1
Parents unknown	9	Failed in Business	5
Father drowned on his passage to this country	1	Parents in Europe	2
Emigrants newly arrived	3		
Mothers keeping girls and can't lodge boys			2
Fathers deserting mothers, and then lodging with other men			5

Our visitors, Mr. Moore Dupuy and Mr. C.C. Tracy, have carefully investigated institutions, prisons, and almshouses for criminal children within and near the City, on Staten Island, in New Jersey, Long Island, and Westchester County. In all cases, the men found one of the prolific causes of crimes involving the boys to be lack of a trade.

The Industrial School Teachers

- The Eleventh Ward School No. 709 East Eleventh Street (held in two rooms of the Boys Lodging House) teachers are Miss A. Van Vorst, Miss Flora Neely, and Miss M. Satterie.

- The East River School No. 206 East Fortieth Street teachers are Mrs. E.S. Hurley, Mrs. Katie Franz, and Miss Ida Hutton.

- The West Sixteenth Street Girls School at No. 120 West Sixteenth Street teachers are Mrs. A. McManus, Miss H. McAneny, and Miss Jones.

- The Hudson River School at No. 350 West Twenty-Seventh Street teachers are Miss L. Noble and Miss F. McAneny.

- The German School at No. 272 Second Street teachers are Miss E. Robertson, Miss A.E. Chandler, Miss A. Strathern, Miss E.S. Lowe, Miss M. Staats, and Mrs. E. Pieligaard.

- The Italian School at No. 44 Franklin Street teachers are Mr. A.E. Cerqua, Mrs. Alleyne, Miss Richards, and Mr. Demartini.

- The Park School at Sixty-Eighth-Street and Broadway teachers are Miss M. Pascali, Miss S. Robinson, Miss H. Taylor, and Miss Birdsall.

- The Fifty-Second Street School (near Eleventh Avenue) teachers are Miss E. Bishop and Miss J. Mallory.

- The Fifty-Third Street School (shares the German Lutheran Church) at No. 340 West Fifty-Third Street teachers are Miss S. Seymour, Miss M. Johnson, Miss E.A. Bayliss, and Miss F. Coleman.

- The Fifth Ward School at No. 141 Hudson Street teachers are Miss M.E. Mallory and Miss A. Marsh.

- The Phelps School at No. 335 East Thirty-Fifth Street teachers are Miss S.S. Parsons and Miss S. Allen.

- The Thirteenth Ward School at No. 327 Rivington Street teachers are Miss E. Phillips, Miss A. Johnson and Miss Alburtis.

- The Fourth Ward School at No. 52 Market Street teachers are Miss M. Dunn and Miss J. Dunn.

- The Sixteenth Ward School at No. 211 West Eighteenth Street teachers are Miss Haight and Miss Jackson.

- The Cottage Place School at No. 204 Bleecker Street (in the old factory building started by Mr. Macy) teachers are Mrs. Foreman, Miss E. Wells, Miss N. Hogan, and Miss S. Todd.

- Lord School at No. 207 Greenwich Street teachers are Miss S. Flagg and Miss N. Randolph.

- Avenue B School at No. 607 East Fourteenth Street teachers are Miss Jane Andrews and Miss Kate Collard.

- The Fourteenth Ward School at No. 93 Crosby Street teachers are Miss H.E. Stevens, Miss E.S. Stevens, Miss N. McGrath, and Miss S. Hollis.

- Eighth Ward School (colored pupils) at No. 185 Spring Street and Newsboy's Evening School at No. 49 Park Place.

- Trustees of the Children's Aid Society during 1871 are Messrs. Benjamin J. Howland, Howard Potter, Horatio Allen, Theodore Roosevelt, and A. Van Rensselaer.

BRACE MEMORIAL FARM SCHOOL

The New York Times
December 5, 1894

Credit: The New York Times page 3.
Brace Memorial Farm School

Newsboys and Bootblacks of New York Trained for Western Homes — Success of the Scheme.

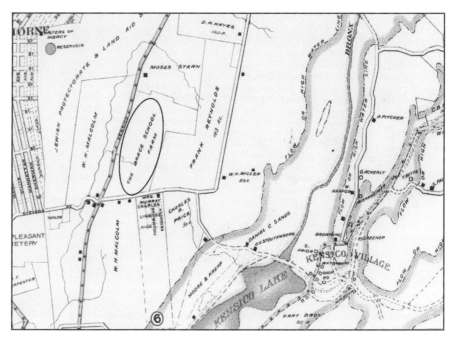

Kensico in Westchester County, New York, 1908. The Brace Farm School.
David Rumsey Map Collection.

Thirty five miles from New York City on the line of the New York Central and Hudson River Railroad lay the peaceful hamlet of Kensico. If one takes a short drive in an easterly direction of Kensico and inquires for the Newsboys Farm, he will probably find a spot where he can spend a few hours free of monotony.

Two years ago the fact that so many bootblacks and newsboys, sent to farmers in the West and South, turned out substandard with difficulty to their employers, was brought to the attention of Mrs. Joseph M. White, an active worker in the Children's Aid Society of New York City. With the advice of C.L. Brace, secretary of the society, Mrs. White determined a new plan for benefitting the boys, and presented a sum of money sufficient to erect a new building in 1894.

On a high plateau 600 feet above sea level, and within two miles of Kensico is situated a tract of fertile land containing 125 acres, an old fashioned manor, a barn, a springhouse, and all the equipment of a well regulated farm. The property was bought, and donated to the society by Mrs. White.

Soon repairs had been made, and twenty street Arabs from the Newsboys Lodging House on Chambers Street in New York City were taken to the farm at their own request, and were charmed with the idea of sleeping on a real bed every night without pay. There has never been any difficulty in keeping the ranks replenished.

The purpose of the farm is to give practical farm instructions to boys ten to sixteen years old, so when they are provided with homes on Western farms, they

may be of immediate value and service. It is in short, a probation school. Every boy is given a six weeks trial. If he proves to be of good material and trustworthy, he is sent out West. Should he turn out ineffectual, he is sent back to New York, and may have another trial. Thus far there have been very few of the latter kind.

The new structure stands on an eminence square in shape. The general colonial exterior design includes a broad porch with columns and a balcony, along with wide spread eaves. The architects of the building were Vaux and Emery of New York, and they have shown unusual judgment in their work, as the building meets every possible requirement.

A particularly wise provision on the first floor consisted of a lavatory, and washroom. The interior encompassed in finished pine eludes exceptional radiance. Every boy keeps in his locker a pair of slippers, which he dons before entering into the main part of the house.

All vehicles were pressed into service today by the many patrons of the society, who were anxious to inspect the new building. As each carriage entered the private lane of the farm, the quondam newsboys and bootblacks, lined their baseball field, and greeted everyone with a chorus of yells mingled with Bowery slang.

Superintendents at the Brace Memorial Farm School in 1900 were Floyd Goff, and in 1905-1910 Charles P. Fischer who worked for the Children's Aid Society eleven years prior. The three settlements of Kensico, Wright Mills, and Davis Brook once comprised present day Valhalla in Westchester County, New York.

Besides the Farm Training School for boys in Kensico, Westchester County, New York, the work of the Children's Aid Society included the summer charities of the Children's Summer Home, Haxtun Cottage for Crippled Girls at Bath Beach, Long Island, and Health Home at West

Coney Island. The industrial and night schools were approachable for those who could not attend public schools. A number of early locations include:

Industrial Schools:
- Avenue B, 533 East Sixteenth Street
- Beach Street, 36 Beach Street
- Duane Street, 9 Duane Street
- East River, 247 East Forty-Fourth Street
- East Side, 287 East Broadway (included Sick Children's Mission and East Side Flower Mission)
- Fifty-Second Street, 573 West Fifty-Second Street
- German, 272 Second Street
- Henrietta, 215 East Twenty-First Street
- Italian, 156 Leonard Street
- Jones Memorial, 407 East Seventy-Third Street
- Lord Memorial, 173 Rivington Street
- Mott Street, 256 Mott Street
- Phelps, 314 East Thirty-Fifth Street
- Pike Street, 28 Pike Street
- Rhinelander, 350 East Eighty-Eighth Street
- Sixth Street, 630 Sixth Street
- Sixty-Fourth Street, 207 West Sixty-Fourth Street

- Sullivan Street, 219 Sullivan Street (included free reading rooms in addition to each lodge house)
- Tompkins Square, 295 Eighth Street
- West Side, 201 West Thirty-Second Street (included Boy's Printing Office)
- West Side Italian, 24 Sullivan Street

Night Schools:
- Bearley League, 552 West Fifty-Third Street
- East Side, 287 East Broadway
- Elizabeth Home for Girls, 307 East Twelfth Street (included sewing, dress-making, typewriting, and laundry)
- Forty-Fourth Street, 247 East Forty-Fourth Street
- German, 272 Second Street
- Henrietta, 215 East Twenty-First Street
- Italian, 156 Leonard Street
- Jones Memorial, 407 East Seventy-Third Street
- Newsboys, 9 Duane Street
- Sullivan Street, 219 Sullivan Street
- Tompkins Square, 295 East Eighth Street
- West Side, 201 West Side Thirty-Second Street
- West Sixty-fourth Street, 207 West Sixty-Fourth Street

The New York Times
January 15, 1896

Credit: The New York Times page 9. Starting For New Homes; Farm Training School Children Sent West and South. Well Clothed Before Departing. How the Boys and Girls Are Provided For - The Six Months at the Farm to Develop Their Characters

Agents Anna Laura Hill and B.W. Tice escorted these new arrivals to Lebanon, Missouri, in 1909. They are waiting to be chosen.

The Children's Aid Society Collection.

Forty to fifty boys and girls arrived at 9 o'clock from the Farm Training School at Kensico in Westchester County. Each boy was examined by a physician, and pronounced in good physical condition.

The happy sturdy looking lot took three trains yesterday to Unionville, Missouri; Garnet, Kansas; and Jacksonville, Florida.

They are boys who have no parents, or whose parents are unable to support them, and have relinquished all claim upon them when the Society takes them in hand. One boy stated, "Mother works out, and gives up all claim." As for thoughts on the Farm School, and their new adventure, "It was just a holiday to me at the time I was at the Brace School. I was there six months, and I am going south. I think they will take us ten miles from Jacksonville. I don't know how I shall like it. I have never been further South then Washington before. I saw Coxey's army then. Such a lot of rowdies, and they made a regular General out of Coxey, who rode around with a yellow sash." Another commented, "I have been in Kansas. My aunt has a farm there, and after my father and mother died, I went out there, and stayed for a time. I saw one prairie fire. The

western part of Kansas is a bad place to live in. You starve there, and have to beg for something to eat.

"These fellows are going to the eastern part of Kansas, and it is better there. There is lots of corn in Kansas. There is not much shade, and no chestnut trees. I think you could get $17 a bushel for chestnuts in Kansas. There are plenty of hickory nuts though." Turning to a young lad a visitor remarked, "You will be able to eat oranges fresh from the trees in Florida," "Not now," mentioned the boy, "There have been such bad frosts, that there will not be any oranges for a couple of years."

"This society's awful rich,"

said a small lad by the name of Louis, in the rooms of the Children's Aid Society in the United Charities Building yesterday morning. Then he gazed down the length of himself admiringly. From head to foot he was newly clothed. New hat, new shoes, and a brand new natty looking overcoat surmounted a new suit of clothing. "We all got new underclothes too," the boy said.

Louis noted that his younger sister Minnie was, "going by a lady." The meaning behind the comment interprets to a woman in the West has opened the doors of her home, and it is to be hoped of her heart, that little Minnie is going to live with her. "There are not many children going with Mr.

Tice," Minnie said. She and her brother Louis were among the smallest of the children who went West. The younger boys went South.

There was a pathetic side to the scene; all to these homeless children starting for new homes in the West must begin their lives with strangers. Mrs. Joseph M. White was present at the Society to see another group of beneficiaries of her work off for new homes. She produced a package of bright colored Testaments, and gave them to each boy who could read, and who wished them. Most of the boys did, and the books were gone before all the boys had been supplied.

The New York Times
November 29, 1899

Credit: The New York Times page 8. Children's Aid Society; Its Vast Work Made Public at the Annual Meeting

The Children's Aid Society Not Only Places Children, But Finds Homes For Men And Women

The 47th Annual Report of the Children's Aid Society reports the industrial schools attendance profile achieved 7,218 pupils during the year, with an enrollment of 15,773. The teachers have made 17,097 visits to the homes of children, and 799 truants have been brought in. Appearing in parts of the City, especially in the lower east side districts, children are growing up entirely neglected.

The number of homeless boys and girls seeking shelter in our lodging houses has reached 4,217, and we have placed 294 with families in the country, 941 have been adopted into homes, or they are on trial for adoption. The boys and girls put into situations (work) outside the City totals 304. An important feature in the removal of destitute men and women who are unable to make their own living here, is to help place them in other parts of the United States, where friends and family will care for them, and where they can seek employment. An example is compared to a woman with small children who has suffered the loss of her husband; she is financially, spiritually, and physically in an ominous dilemma. She may have a relative or friend living in California, and as a result, the Children's Aid Society will help assist her and the children to their destination. This year, 943 men and women have been sent to friends for care, and employment in the country. The total number of individuals sent away from the overcrowded City during the eleven months of this year was 1,571.

In the past thirty years (since 1854) the Children's Aid Society has received 70,000 children who are in need of assistance. In the first twenty years 20,000 children were placed in permanent country homes with more than 2,000 under the age of ten. Those that have been received from parents or relatives add up to 6,118, the rest are from the lodge houses, industrial schools, and private establishments. Most adolescents are now farmers, or are involved in various lines of business. Two have become governors, one a district commissioner, one a sheriff, and one a congressman.

John Brady

Andrew Burke

EXECUTIVE STREET BOYS

In 1918 the New York Times reported that John (James) Green Brady, Alaska's Executive Governor for three terms, was a former ward of the Children's Aid Society. At the age of eight he had sold newspapers, shined shoes, ran errands, carried satchels to the steamboat docks, and canvassed the East River water front in the hope of picking up odd jobs. "Johnny" often slept curled up in a box or in some dark street corner. One night he was picked up by a policeman and sent with a boatload of other waifs to Randall's Island. In the summer of 1859, the Children's Aid Society arranged to send a large number of the boys to the West, and among them was Brady, relegated to the home of John Green, a leading lawyer of Tipton, Indiana.

On the same orphan train as Brady was an eight-year-old lad named Andrew H. Burke, consigned to a farmer in Noblesville, Indiana. Burke's mother had died at his birth and his father died four years later. He fell under the care of the Children's Aid Society as reported in an 1892 New York Times article. At the age of twelve, Andrew ran away from his foster home to join the Civil War, becoming a drummer boy for the Seventy-Fifth Indiana Volunteers. In 1880, Burke went to Casselton, North Dakota to work at a bank in a treasurer's position. In 1890, Andrew Burke was nominated and elected Governor of North Dakota.

The New York Times
November 27, 1901

Credit: The New York Times page. 9. Years Work of the Children's Aid Society; Forty-Ninth Annual Report

The 49th report of the Children's Aid Society ended last October 1st. The meeting began with the election of officers. William Church Osborn was elected President, taking the place of D. Willis James who has held the office since 1892. Mr. James continues as trustee. Charles E. Whitehead as Vice President; A. Barton Hepburn as Treasurer, and Charles Loring Brace (son of the founder) as Secretary. Elected trustees to serve a three year term are William Douglas Sloane, F. Delano Weekes, and Archibald D. Russell.

A new Italian Industrial School was proposed by the Society, with a location in Little Italy on the upper east side, an extension at the Children's Summer Home for crippled children is needed, and improvements at the Farm School.

The emigration and placing out department notes the Superintendent of Emigration is Robert N. Brace. During the year, 407 children were placed in family homes, mainly in the West. There are now 972 children ages

Newsies selling on the Capitol steps in Washington, D.C., 1912.
Lewis Hine Collection. Library of Congress.

sixteen or younger in homes of farm families under the supervision of the Society. Agents of the Society have paid 1,355 visits to the children through the year to learn of their welfare. Sent to situations (work) with country families for wages were 263 older boys and girls, and 589 parents with children were aided to reach employment in various states. 144 runaway boys were retuned to their parents. In all, 1,403 destitute children were placed in country homes during the year.

The summer charities of the Society were bountiful. The Children's Summer Home at Bath Beach was crowed from June to September. 285 crippled children each spent two weeks at the Haxtun Cottage. The Health Home at Coney Island was full to capacity with 3,318 young sufferers sent from dispensaries each staying one week. 2,079 tenement boys at the Farm School Cottage were given a week's outing.

The New York Times
November 26, 1902

Credit: The New York Times page 5.
Rescue of Little Ones

Newsboys reading room in Boston, Massachusetts, with boys engaged in recreation in 1909.

Lewis Hine Collection. Library of Congress.

The meeting of the Children's Aid Society officers met at the Chase National Bank [meetings were often held at the Chase or Metropolitan banks] marked the completion of Fifty Years of activity on the part of the Society in this City. C. Loring Brace, son of the founder Charles Loring Brace of this Society declared: "No poor child in New York need be homeless on the street, nor be forced to neither steal or beg for a living, nor want a meal, if he gives evidence that he is willing to work for it." Brace went on to give the statistical numbers of the children added to the Children's Aid Society's tabulations, "Those who are in the Industrial Schools total 16,364, Home relief has been given to 9,307, in our Lodging Houses we have 4,226 tenants, 645 boys at the Farm School are learning farming skills, those who are under the charge of probation officers counts up to 300, there are 10,562 persons in the Summer Homes, those treated by the Sick Mission adds up to 1,486, and those given outings equal 1,761. We have placed 476 in Western homes, and 247 have been placed in homes at wages. Folks that have been assisted to emigrate collectively reach 712, reaching 55,106 people the Society has helped.

Mr. Brace went on to say, "The principle of the Society is to give the children of the poor and unfortunate, the means of self help, and to encourage them to use the means. We find in all kinds of humanity a divinity given uplifting power, stronger than the down pulling influences of heredity. Remove the child from bad environments before the age when instincts are polluted, and place him amid good family surroundings. He will develop naturally in the discipline of every day life, and will grow in moral health and strength, exactly as the average child does."

FATHER JOHN C. DRUMGOOLE

Crredit: Mount Loretto, Staten Island excerpts

John C. Drumgoole
*Mount Loretto, Staten Island,
New York Collection.*

John Christopher Drumgoole was born in County Longford in 1816 and came to New York City as an Irish immigrant boy, later working as a sexton for St. Mary's Church on Grand Street of the Lower East Side. As poverty was prevalent, he permitted children of the street to gather in the church's basement for shelter. Within one square mile of lower Manhattan, 290,000 people were packed in to filthy tenements.

Typhus, yellow fever, cholera, and diphtheria swept throughout the municipality, wiping out thousands. The city dumps continued to provide the main source of food for hundreds. Homeless children ran rampant in the streets, and hundreds were already confirmed alcoholics or involved in petty crimes. The children roamed the streets at night with no options for sanctuary.

At the age of fifty-three, Drumgoole was ordained a priest, living at 246 East Broadway in New York City. He ministered to the homeless boys of the street and took over St. Vincent's Home for Homeless Boys in 1870. The home took in boys of all occupations (bootblacks, newsboys, rag and bottle pickers, etc.) at No. 53 Warren Street, and Drumgoole was appointed chaplain director of the Society of St. Vincent de Paul.

The shelter, an old warehouse, was situated only a few blocks from Newspaper Row or Printing House Square [the newspaper headquarters established two blocks east from the World Trade Center site, and directly across from City Hall, was the heart of the American press for fifty years.]

Having grown up impoverished, the priest understood the challenges faced by the New York newsboys, and he worked hard to let them know about the shelter. He posted fliers and searched for the homeless children in dark alleyways, under bridges, and in the places that newsboys lived when not selling papers. The shelter accepted only homeless working boys and offered evening school classes, plus safe lodging for a small fee with free dinners on Sundays. Father John lived with the boys doing exactly what he wanted to do with his life. Nothing was as significant to his heart as the welfare of his children.

Protestant, Catholic, and civic authorities did what they could to solve the insurmountable problems of homeless and impoverished children. Charles Loring Brace, founder of the Children's Aid Society, had suggested his plan of moving children to foster homes in the American West, where farmers, families, and manufacturers would value children's labor. Brace hoped that adoptions would eventually materialize, and the children would attain a better life.

Drumgoole met with a company of children who were to be shipped West. Since authorities made no attempt to match the religion of the foster home with a child, the plan was not looked upon favorably by Catholics. The clergyman protested. He deemed the idea unlawful, as some of the transports he knew were Catholic children of poor, respectable, and industrious widows, who faithfully paid board to the institution to prevent their children from being separated from faith and family. The priest was requested to claim responsibility for the children, as they could no longer remain at the city institution. Drumgoole sheltered the little band in his Newsboys Home while sending for their mothers. The mothers were wild with grief, thinking their child had been sent west. Members of the group in question were under nine years of age, and some were under four. The priest found foster homes for those with no families and provided financial support for those who welcomed the children into their midst. Drumgoole felt the children's quandary was "New York's problem, and we have the resources to solve it." At times, children were left at hospitals with no identification of creed and were doled out to orphanages in random fashion. Drumgoole fought consistently and eventually successfully for the passage of legislation protecting the religious rights of children who were transported to the West if their faith preference was known.

By 1873 the priest was successful in attracting boys to the home by putting out a paper called "The Homeless Child" to obtain a source of income. He started the St Joseph's Union for the support of the institution and eventually extended its membership all over the world. The building on Warren Street was soon filled to capacity, so the priest purchased land and built a ten-story shelter in December of 1881, calling it the Newsboys Home. This building was located at the corner of New York's Great Jones Street and Lafayette Place, opening as the Mission of the Immaculate Virgin for the Protection of Homeless and Destitute Children.

The Vincentians raised $4,000 to rent and refurbish a loft building next to the original structure. Once converted the basement held a kitchen and a hundred-gallon tank for cooking soup for residents and the poor of the neighborhood. The chapel and administrative offices were located on the first floor, classrooms and libraries on the second and living quarters on the upper floors. The roof, enclosed in mesh, was the first rooftop playground in New York City. The priest owed not one penny on the building, and in the early 1880s even managed to obtain a mansion in Fort Washington on the eastern shore of the Hudson River, as an ideal place for girls who were orphaned.

In June of 1882, the priest bought three farms totaling 250 acres located on Staten Island. He named it Mount Loretto, after a town in Italy. This new purchase eventually accommodated homeless working boys and girls. The female residents from Fort Washington were moved to Mount Loretto where they received care from the Franciscan Sisters. An infant home was attached to Mount Loretto, and children were schooled by some of the finest educators of the time. By 1886, 1,180 children were divided equally between Mount Loretto and the "city house" in Manhattan.

Farming operations at Mount Loretto came under the control of former newsboys. Children plowed fields, milked cows, cared for horses, and made their own clothes and shoes. St. Joseph's Trade School was added, offering courses in printing, shoemaking, harness and press work, typesetting, carpentry, tailoring, woodworking, plumbing, machine maintenance and operations, gardening, floral designing, navigation, and typing and stenography. Father Drumgoole implemented an employment agency, placing many of his boys in city shops, industries, professions and trades. Alumni of this institution held ranks as priests, doctors, lawyers, professors, artists, musicians, and in other vocations. Drumgoole followed this rule: "by looking after the interests of the child, it is necessary to cultivate the heart."

Pope Leo XIII, a good friend of Don Bosco, who had worked successfully with thousands of Italian youth, once asked Drumgoole to visit him at the Vatican and explain the work he had done for American youth. Though the priest admired the pope, he regretted turning down the invitation, as his calendar was full of activities related to his vocation. Instead, he arranged an album of photographs depicting the buildings, priests, staff, and children and sent the book to the

The Mission of the Immaculate Virgin was completed in 1881. The Franciscan Sisters, under Father Drumgoole's guidance, administered to hundreds of children who called this building home.

Mount Loretto, Staten Island, New York Collection.

The statue of Father John Drumgoole with newsboys. Sculptor Robert Cushing, New York City.

Mount Loretto, New York Collection.

Holy Father. In return Drumgoole received a letter stating, "May God shower down on you, on your missioners, on your children, and on all your work, the abundance of His grace, and the spirit of His heart. Our missioners, our poor orphans, all of us, shall pray for you, especially during the Holy Sacrifice of the Mass, but let a continued exchange of prayer pass between the Old Europe and the Young America, for the glory of God, and the salvation of souls.

Your very humble servant in Christ, abbe. J. Bosco."

Saint Don Bosco, born Giovanni Melchiorre Bosco, and known in English as John Bosco; was declared Blessed in 1929, and a Saint on Easter Sunday in 1934. He was given the title of "Father and Teacher of Youth."

Father Drumgoole never failed to commute each day to Manhattan to make entrusted deposits in the New York Emigrant Savings Bank or to spend time with the newsboys. He happened to get caught up in the Great March Blizzard of 1888, from which he contracted pneumonia. The priest was urged to go to St. Vincent's Hospital, but he refused. Several years earlier, a severe cold had worn him out. This time, doctors announced that he had suffered from pneumonia for too long and their assistance was hindered because he was so weak.

Death came to Father John C. Drumgoole during Easter Holy Week on the evening of March 28, 1888, at the age of seventy-two. Through Drumgoole's death, the boys lost their best friend. It is estimated that 100,000 people came to pay their respects at the priest's funeral. The Mass at St. Patrick's Cathedral was filled to capacity, with thousands of poor and hundreds of priests and bishops. Father John is buried at Mount Loretto on Staten Island with "his children."

A memorial statue was erected and placed in front of the Mission at Lafayette Street in Manhattan in 1894. The statue remained there for twenty- five years before being relocated to Staten Island in 1920. The statue portrays Father Drumgoole with two boys. One boy is well dressed and reading a book; the other is a ragged newsboy who has thrown down his pack of papers and clings to the priest for protection. The two figures represent the same boy before and after meeting Father John Drumgoole. [On April 16, 1894 page 3 of The New York Times reported that the boy on the statue was inspired by a little City Hall Park bootblack named "Pat" who boarded at Drumgoole's home in Warren Street.]

Family

We define the word in various ways
Mom, dad, sister, and brother,
Conceiving and receiving the children we raise
A social unit living together.

Families make you feel comfortable
Individuals you love and enjoy,
Loving unconditionally acceptable
Tender caring for a girl or boy.

Love, courage, strength, and weakness
Support, forgiveness, and tears,
Making somebody's life better – not less
Soothing away the fears.

Family is the greatest bond
A comforting feeling where you belong,
Remaining a part of your life beyond
An element linked together strong.

What makes a family is not just DNA
It is unity no matter what the relation,
Connecting in a meaningful way
A heart-loving sensation.

© 2008 Renée Wendinger

VOCABULARY

Abandoned– a: to give up to the control or influence of another person or agent;
b: give up with the intent of never again claiming a right or interest.

Adolescence– the state or process of growing up, or the period of life from puberty to maturity.

Adopted– to take by choice into a relationship; especially to take voluntarily a child of other parents as one's own child.

Advertisement– the act or process of calling something to the attention of the public as in a notice, flyer, or ad; especially published in the press.

Agent– one who is authorized to act for or in the place of another; as a representative.

Baby Train– the New York Foundling Hospital orphanage often called the trains their children rode "baby trains" or "mercy trains," since many babies through age six rode them.

Bier– a stand on which a corpse or coffin is placed.

Biological– connected by direct genetic relationship rather than by adoption or marriage in life.

Bootblack– one who shines shoes.

Borough– one of the five administrative divisions of New York City: Manhattan (New York County), Bronx (Bronx County), Queens (Queens County), Brooklyn (Kings County), Staten Island (Richmond County) make up the five boroughs of New York City.

Bowery– a city district known for cheap bars and derelicts; a street in New York City.

Bummer– a: a loafer or one who bums;
b: not occupied or employed.

Car– a vehicle designed to move on rails (as of a railroad); the orphan train children traveled in cars.

Chosen– a person who is the object of choice or favor; elected.

Chronicles– records, archives, history.

Company– a group of persons; a company of children sent west on an orphan train.

Descendant– proceeding from an ancestor or source as in offspring, child, or successor.

Emigration– to leave one's place of residence or country to live elsewhere.

Family– a group of persons of common ancestry; the basic unit in society traditionally consisting of two parents rearing their children; various social units differing from, but regarded as equivalent to the traditional family.

Foster– to receive, nurture, or apply parental care though not related by blood or legal ties.

Foundling– an infant found after its unknown parents have abandoned it.

Immigration– to enter and usually become established; especially to come into a country of which one is not a native for permanent residence.

Indenture– a: a contract binding one person to work for another for a given period of time
b: a document stating the terms under which a security is issued.

Lodge House– a house or building used as a temporary shelter or residence for newsboys, boot blacks, messenger boys, and young vendors in place of doorways, cellars, and streets.

Messenger– an employee who carries messages (a communication in writing) to others.

Migration– to move from one country, place, or locality to another.

Neglected– to give little attention or respect; to leave unattended through carelessness.

Newsboy– one who delivers or sells newspapers to earn money for survival; the newsboys were referred to as "newsies," or "newsys," meaning full of news.

Orphan– a child deprived by death of one or usually both parents. Also, orphanage– an institution for the care of orphans.

Orphan Train– during 1854–1929 approximately 250,000 orphaned or abandoned children of various ages rode on trains from New York to all points west across the United States in an effort to find a family and home.

Orphan Train Rider– the orphaned or abandoned children from New York who rode the trains.

Pauper– a person without means of support; a very poor person.

Placed Out– to direct to a desired spot, place, or destination.

Potter's Field– a place to bury unclaimed strangers or paupers who died indigent.

Poverty– a: the state of one with insufficient resources; b: the state of one who lacks a usual or socially acceptable amount of money or material possessions.

Prospective– in the future, likely to be, become, or come about, as in prospective parents.

Relinquish– a: to give over possession or control of; b: withdraw or retreat from, to leave behind, as in relinquish a child to an orphanage.

West– a common term East Coast orphanages and the press used when an orphan train departed to any state west of New York. The midwestern states were frequent destinations.

SOURCE CITATIONS :
IMAGES AND PICTURES

Book Cover: Orphan Train, purchased photo and permission rights from the Kansas State Historical Society, 6425 South West Sixth Avenue, Topeka, Kansas 66615. Newsboy's photo from the Library of Congress; photograph use under the Child Labor Committee commissioned for a government agency.

Book Cover Flipside: Homeless and Friendless 1891; T.P. Sperry.

The Children's Aid Society Archive, New York, New York. Permission acquired: archivists Lammers and Remer; retrieval 1980s, 1990s.

Orphan Train for Texas, 1904. (pg. v)

Boys in front of the Children's Aid Society building bound for Missouri, 1908. (pg. 11, 82)

Charles Loring Brace. (pg. 13)

Advertisement- Children Want Homes. (pg. 14)

Advertisement- Homes Wanted for Children, 1907. (pg. 15)

Agent H.D. Clarke. (pg. 16)

Agents Hill & Tice with Children, 1910. (pg. 16, 156)

Orphan Train Bound for Texas, 1904. (pg. 51)

The Newsboys of New York. (pg. 81, 112)

Brace Memorial Lodge House. (pg. 97)

News Boys Lodge House on No. 9 Duane Street. (pg. 100)

Christmas Dinner at a Newsboys Lodge New York, New York. (pg. 120)

Italian School, New York, New York. (pg. 144)

The New York Foundling Hospital New York, New York.
Permission acquired archivist Sister Marilda Joseph; retrieval 1998.

The New York Foundling Hospital on Sixty-eighth and Lexington Street. (pg. 12)

Sister Irene, 1896. (pg. 17)

First Home of the New York Foundling Hospital, 1869. (pg. 17)

Second Home of the New York Foundling Hospital, 1870. (pg. 18)

New York Foundling Hospital Buildings, 1873. (pg. 19)

Historical Cradle. (pg. 20)

Sister Teresa Vincent, 1917. (pg. 21)

Sister Teresa Vincent Accepting Infant. (pg. 21)

Tagged Babies in Netted Crib. (pg. 22)

Fourth Home of the New York Foundling Hospital, 1958. (pg. 23)

Children getting dressed. (pg. 38)

The World; Children Leaving the Foundling, 1912. (pg. 42)

Children of the Foundling Ready to Board, Al Appleton, 1923. (pg. 43)

The Evening World; New York's Christmas Gifts, 1918. (pg. 44)

The World; Real Fathers and Mothers Are Christmas Gifts For These Babies, December 11, 1918. (pg. 45)

Seton Hospital Nazareth, 1880s. (pg. 46)

George Abel Prize Foundling. (pg. 58)

National Orphan Train Complex, Concordia, Kansas,
http://www.orphantrainriders.com.

Policeman with Baby. (pg. 19)

Orphan Train State Map. (pg. 34)

Children going to Lebanon, Missouri with Agents Hill and Tice. (pg. 155)

Minnesota Historical Society Research Center, St. Paul, Minnesota. Acquired 1997.

St. Paul Union Depot. (pg. 37)

The Dominican Sisters, Congregation of St. Mary New Orleans. Permission acquisition archivist/historian Sister Dorothy Dawes, New Orleans, Louisiana, acquired 2007, 2009.

Sarah Hunt, 1909. (pg. 39)

Library of Congress Prints and Photographs Division, Washington, D.C. 20540 USA. Prints & Photographs Online Catalog-PPOC.

The entire collection is assisted by the National Child Labor Committee photographs. No known restrictions applied to publications.

http://hdl.loc.gov/loc.pnp/pp.print.

Children Making Shoes at the Juvenile Asylum; Bain Collection. LC-B22- 331-6[P&P] - Reproduction Number: LC-DIG-ggbain-01563. (pg. 48)

Grand Central Station, New York, New York, 1895. Railroad Stations, A.P Yates. U.S. GEOG FILE [P&P] - Reproduction Number: LC-USZ62-74617. (pg. 52)

The Newsboy, May 31, 1922. SSF–Child Labor—Newsboys. [P&P]- Reproduction Number: LC-USZ62-73857PPOC. (pg. 83)

Funeral from Tenement House in Baxter Street, Five Points. Frank Leslie's illustrated newspaper, v. 20 (July 1, 1865) pg. 225. [P&P]- Reproduction number: LC-USZ62-121734 b & w Illus. AP2.L52 1865 (Case Y). (pg. 117)

Boy Looking at Christmas Toys in Shop Window. George Grantham Bain Collection. [P&P] - LC-B2- 941-13. (pg. 124)

Newspaper War Bulletins, Park Row, New York City, 1898. R. Y. Young Collection. P&P] - LOT 12300-1. (pg. 128)

At the Side Door of the Journal Building Near the Brooklyn Bridge, February, 1908. [P&P]- LOT 7480, v. 1, no. 0018-A. (pg. 129)

Poker Game in the "Den of the Terrible Nine" waiting Room for Western Union Messenger's, Hartford, Connecticut, March 1909. [P&P]- LOT 4780, v. 1, no. 0592. (pg. 130)

Group of Newsboys on Frankfort Street near the World Building, New York, February 1908. [P&P]- LOT 7480, v.1, no. 0033-A. (pg. 133)

An Afternoon with Some of Newark's Newsboys, 1909. [P&P]- LOT 7480, v. 1, no. 1034. (pg. 134)

Newsies starting out with Sunday papers, 6 A.M. Boston, Massachusetts, October 1909. [P&P]-LOT 7480, v. 1, no. 0879. (pg. 146)

Group of Newsies Selling on Capitol Steps in Washington (D.C.) District of Columbia, April 11, 1912. [P&P]- LOT 7480, v. 3 no. 2905. (pg. 159)

Newsboys Reading Room. LOT 7480, v. 1, no. 0949 [P&P] - LC-H5- 949. (pg. 160)

Newsboys and Girls in Hartford, Connecticut, 1909. [P&P]- LOT 7480, V. 1, no. 0662. (pg. 171)

Library of Congress Prints and Photographs Division, Washington, D.C. 20540 USA. Prints & Photographs Online Catalog-PPOC. Jacob Riis Collection of the National Child Labor Committee (U.S.) Unrestricted rights from a government agency. Newspaper boys.

Newsboy in the Duane Street Lodging House, 1889. LOT 6300 [P&P] - Reproduction number: LC-USZ62-57744. (pg. 84)

Boys sleeping on doorsteps in New York City, 1888. LOT 6300 [P&P] - Reproduction number: LC-USZ62-39057. (pg. 93)

"Washing up" in the newsboys' lodging house, 1890. LOT 6300 [P&P] - Reproduction number: LC-USZ62-16347. (pg. 98)

The George Eastman House, Rochester, New York. Lewis Wickes Hine purchased photographs.

Greek Bootblacks, New York City, 1906. GEH NEG: 3762; Reproduction number: 77:0179:0004. (pg. 89)

Newsies and Bootblacks shooting craps, 1910. GEH NEG: 33766; Reproduction number 77:0179:0008. (pg. 91)

Candid Shot of Newsie Selling Papers on Street, 1912. GEH NEG: 30161; Reproduction number: 77:0178:0006. (pg. 141)

The City Museum of New York, New York. Jacob Riis purchased photographs.

Mulberry Street, New York City, New York, 1890. (pg. 92)

Boys sleeping on a steam grate in the New York Sun office. (pg. 106)

Church corner sleeping area on Mulberry Street New York City. (pg. 107)

"Don't Live Nowhere." (pg. 109)

@ Bettmann/CORBIS purchased photograph.

The New York Juvenile Asylum Sunday School in the Village, 1938. (pg. 49)

The Statue of Liberty, landmarks of New York, public domain. (pg. 50)

Grand Forks division map, public domain. (pg. 69)

United States map, New York to Nebraska, public domain. (pg. 77)

Printing House Square, public domain. (pg. 84)

Horatio Alger, public domain. (pg. 103)

Newsboys assembling papers for the New York Sun, Anonymous. (pg. 104)

Homeless New York street boys. Darkness and Daylight of New York, Helen Campbell, personal collection. (pg. 112)

John Brady and Andrew Burke, public domain. (pg. 158)

Waiting for the train, public domain. (pg. 179)

David Rumsey Map Collection, permission use authorized.

1908 Kensico map, [E. Becker Hyde]. (pg. 154)

Kansas State Historical Society; Topeka, Kansas. Purchased photograph and permission rights acquired January 2008.

Kansas Orphan Train Panoramic. (pg. 1, 9, 51)

Orphan Train Riders from New York. Signed contract rights acquired in 2007-08. (pg. 53- 79)

© Dorling Kindersley Images London, United Kingdom. Purchased photograph rights.

Italian boy playing the triangle. (pg. 79)

Diana Serra Cary Collection, permission acquisition 2007-08.

Cake cutting with New York Foundling orphans, 1923. (pg. 80)

Written and signed commentary to the New York orphan train riders, November 18, 2007. (pg. 80)

Mount Loretto, Staten Island, New York. Collection, acquisition, 2007.

John C. Drumgoogle. (pg. 161)

Mission of the Immaculate Virgin building. (pg. 163)

Father Drumgoole Statue. (pg. 164)

Author photograph ©Renée Wendinger (pg. 176)

Newsboys and girls in 1909, Hartford, Connecticut.

Lewis Hine Collection. Library of Congress.

SOURCE CITATIONS: TEXT

NATIONAL ORPHAN TRAIN COMPLEX, CONCORDIA, KANSAS, HTTP://WWW.ORPHANTRAINRIDERS.COM.

CHILDREN WANT HOMES. (PG 14)

HOMES WANTED FOR HOMELESS CHILDREN, 1917. (PG. 15)

AGENTS OF THE CHILDREN'S AID SOCIETY AND THE NEW YORK FOUNDLING HOSPITAL. (PG. 15, 16)

HOMES SECURED FOR ORPHAN CHILDREN IN PARIS, ARKANSAS, 1909. (PG. 31)

POEMS: © 2008 RENÉE WENDINGER. (PG. 24, 54, 61, 165)

THE NEW YORK TIMES; NEW YORK, NEW YORK. ARTICLES RETRIEVED FROM PUBLIC DOMAIN ARCHIVE DATABASE PRIOR TO 1923. INCLUSIVE AND PARTIAL TEXT APPLIED WITHIN THIS BOOK'S PROSE.

SISTER MARY IRENE DEAD, AUGUST 15, 1896, PG. 3. (PG. 17)

SISTER TERESA VINCENT; FOUNDLINGS GUARDIAN DIES, MAY 24, 1917, OBITUARY 2, PG. 12. (PG. 21)

HOSPITAL BABIES TAGGED, HOW CONFUSION IS AVOIDED AT DIFFERENT INSTITUTIONS, MAY 20, 1900. (PG. 22)

SENDING FOUNDLINGS WEST; MOTHER SUPERIOR OF THE NEW YORK ASYLUM DEFENDS ROBERT CURRAN AND TELLS OF THE PRACTICE, JUNE 20, 1897, PG. 12. (PG. 32)

NEW YORK ORPHAHS GO WEST; PARTY OF 41 YOUNGSTERS FROM A FOUNDLING ASYLUM REACHES CHICAGO, JULY 10, 1897, PG.2. (PG. 32)

FOUNDLINGS FIND HOMES; CHILDREN FROM CATHOLIC ASYLUMS HERE TAKEN TO THE WEST -- NO RED-HEADED ONES AMONG THEM, MAY 16, 1901, PG. 2. (PG. 34)

FOUNDLINGS SENT TO TEXAS; FIFTY-EIGHT CHILDREN START FOR THE HOMES PROCURED FOR THEM, MAY 10, 1906, PG. 10. (PG. 35)

THE SOUTH CALLS FOR NORTHERN BABIES; FOUNDLING ASYLUM SENT A CARLOAD OF SEVENTY LAST WEEK AND MORE ARE WANTED. TEXAS WRITES TO MAYOR BAPTIST CLERGYMAN AND A FARMER WANT ONE EACH -- ASYLUM'S ORPHANS SENT TO NEW ORLEANS, MARCH 18, 1910, PG. 1. (PG. 40)

FOUNDLINGS SENT WEST; SIXTY-SIX SHIPPED IN A SPECIAL CAR TO HOMES OF FOSTER PARENTS, APRIL 5, 1911, PG. 6. (PG. 41)

FOUNDLINGS SENT WEST; GIRLS IN DEMAND BY THOSE WHO WILL GIVE THEM HOMES, SEPTEMBER 28, 1915 PG. 11- 55. (PG. 43)

REFORMING YOUNG WRONG-DOERS; WORK OF THE NEW-YORK JUVENILE ASYLUM FOR A YEAR, JANUARY 30, 1885, PG. 8. (PG. 48)

NEW YORK JUVENILE ASYLUM, OCTOBER 5, 1871, PG. 8. (PG. 49)

YOUTHFUL EMIGRANTS FOR THE WEST, MARCH 12, 1853, PG. 3; CHARACTER REFERENCES FROM WALKS AMONG THE NEW-YORK POOR; THE NEWS-BOYS, AUGUST 3, 1869, PG. 3. (PG. 49)

WALKS AMONG THE NEW-YORK POOR; THE NEWS-BOYS, MARCH 12, 1854, PG. 3. (PG. 85, 86)

OUT AMONG THE NEWSBOYS; AND A LITTLE CONVERSATION WITH THE BOOTBLACKS. WHY THEY ARE ALL WEARING BLUE CAPS, AUGUST 17, 1879, PG. 5. (PG. 87, 88)

THE CORDIAL RECEPTION OF A BOSTON BOY--CONSUMPTION BROUGHT ON BY BREAD AND MOLASSES. (PG. 88)

CITY HALL PARK STANDS MUST GO; NEWSIES AND BOOTBLACKS WHO HAVE SQUATTED THERE ARE ORDERED OUT. THE "SHINERS" BLAMED "MIKE," "THE COUNT," AND OTHER OLD-TIMERS TAKE THE EVICTION ORDER WITH RESIGNATION, JUNE 15, 1907, PG. 2. (PG. 90)

CHARACTER REFERENCES FROM WALKS AMONG THE NEW-YORK POOR; THE STREET BOYS, SEPTEMBER 28, 1853, PG. 2. (PG. 92, 93)

A RETURNED STREET-BOY'S SPEECH, JANUARY 16, 1875, PG. 8. (PG. 94)

1854--87 THE NEWSBOYS LODGING HOUSES:

AMONG THE NEWSBOYS--LAST SUNDAY EVENING MEETINGS FOR THE SEASON, MAY 9, 1870, PG. 8. (PG. 94)

NEW YORK CITY; THE CHILDREN'S AID SOCIETY. INCENDIARISM. COMMON COUNCIL

PROCEEDINGS. THE TRADES. BOARD OF DOMESTIC MISSIONS OF THE REFORMED DUTCH CHURCH. STEAM DREDGE-BOAT FOR CHARLESTON HAR-ARRANGEMENTS FOR THE FOURTH OF JULY PRISON ASSOCIATION OF NEW-YORK. GRANTING OF LICENSES IN THE TENTH WARD. BODY OF CAPT. JEWETT FOUND, JUNE 28, 1854, PG. 3. (PG. 95)

NEW YORK CITY; THE POLICE DEPARTMENT. THE NEWS-BOYS. THE WEATHER--ITS EFFECTS. THE SHAKERS OF LEBANON. TRINITY METHODIST CHURCH--DEDICATORY EXERCISES, JUNE 30, 1856, PG. 8. (PG. 96)

A NOBLE WORK; ANNUAL MEETING OF THE CHILDREN'S AID SOCIETY. REPORT OF ITS OPERATIONS FOR THE PAST YEAR-WHAT THE SOCIETY HAS BEEN DOING FOR DESTITUTE AND IGNORANT CHILDREN-- NUMBER OF

RESULTS ACHIEVED BY INSTITUTION TRAINING POINTED OUT, NOVEMBER 26, 1902, PG. 5. (PG. 160)

THE NEW YORK FOUNDLING HOSPITAL NEW YORK, NEW YORK. SISTER MARILDA JOSEPH ARCHIVIST, ACQUIRED IN 1998.

EXCERPTS OF THE NEW YORK FOUNDLING HOSPITAL HISTORY. (PG. 17, 18, 19, 20)

NOTICE OF ARRIVAL AND RECEIPT OF CHILD, 1917. (PG. 23)

LETTERS LEFT BY MOTHERS, 1869-84. (PG. 25, 26, 27)

IF YOU'VE EVER TRIED TO DRESS ONE BABY TO TAKE ON A JOURNEY. (PG. 38)

THE WORLD-SIXTY MOTHERLESS BABIES START TO FIND NEW MOTHERS IN THE WEST, 1912. (PG. 41, 42)

100 BABIES, NEW YORK'S CHRISTMAS GIFT TO CHILD HUNGRY HOMES SOUTH AND WEST, 1918. (PG. 44)

THE WORLD- REAL FATHERS AND MOTHERS ARE CHRISTMAS GIFTS FOR THESE BABIES, DECEMBER 11, 1918. (PG. 45, 46)

THIRTY FOUNDLINGS START FOR NEW HOMES IN THE WEST. DATE UNKNOWN. (PG. 46)

THE WORLD- 75 FOUNDLINGS OFF TO FIND HOMES; WILL MEET IN WEST THE FATHERS AND MOTHERS WHOM THEY NEVER HAVE SEEN, JUNE 27, 1917. (PG. 58)

MINNESOTA HISTORICAL SOCIETY RESEARCH CENTER, ST. PAUL, MINNESOTA. RETRIEVED ARTICLES IN 1993.

HOMES FOR THE HOMELESS, JULY 16, 1873, ST. CLOUD TIMES. (PG. 29)

THE SENTINEL, MARTIN COUNTY, OCTOBER 13, 1882. (PG. 29)

COMPANY OF HOMELESS BOYS, FEBRUARY 8, 1888, THE ROCHESTER POST. (PG. 30)

CHILDREN FIND HOMES, JANUARY 13, 1899, MINNEAPOLIS JOURNAL. (PG. 30)

GOING TO HOMES, JUNE 17, 1899 ST. CLOUD TIMES. (PG. 33)

MANY LITTLE ORPHANS, SEPTEMBER 14, 1899, ST. CLOUD TIMES. (PG. 33)

FEARS FOR ORPHANS FATE, AUGUST 22, 1905, MINNEAPOLIS SPECIAL TO WASHINGTON POST. (PG. 35)

A CARLOAD OF BABIES, OCTOBER 15, 1908, ST. PAUL PIONEER. (PG. 36)

ORPHANS FOR ADOPTION, OCTOBER 22, 1909, MINNEAPOLIS JOURNAL. CHILDREN ARE WELCOME. (PG. 36)

DATE UNKNOWN MINNEAPOLIS/ST. PAUL. (PG. 37)

NEW HOMES FOR ORPHANS, NOVEMBER 19, 1913, MINNEAPOLIS JOURNAL. (PG. 43)

A CARLOAD OF ORPHANS FIFTY INFANT ORPHANS HEADS OF CURLY HAIR BOUNCE IN DEPOTS MURKINESS, 1918, ST. PAUL. (PG. 47)

THE DOMINICAN SISTERS ARCHIVES, NEW ORLEANS, LOUISIANA. PERMISSION ACQUIRED FROM ARCHIVIST SISTER DOROTHY DAWES 2007-09.

SARAH HUNT. (PG. 39)

LIBERTY STATE PARK, NEW YORK, N.Y HTTP://WWW.LIBERTYSTATEPARK.COM

THE NEW COLOSSUS. (PG. 50)

ORPHAN TRAIN RIDERS AND THEIR DESCENDANTS, PERMISSION RIGHTS TO BRIEF HISTORIES AND PHOTOGRAPHS THROUGH SIGNED CONTRACTS 2007-08. (PG. 53-79)

PERMISSION ACQUIRED 2007-08 OF IMPARTING EXCERPTS FROM ACTRESS DIANA SERRA CARY (PEGGY LOUISE MONTGOMERY/BABY PEGGY). (PG. 80)

HORATIO ALGER, HTTP://EN.WIKIPEDIA.ORG. (PG 103)

MOUNT LORETTO, STATEN ISLAND, NEW YORK. RETRIEVAL MOUNT LORETTO 2008.

FATHER JOHN DRUMGOOLE EXCERPTS, "LET THE LITTLE CHILDREN COME TO ME." (PG. 161, 162, 163, 164)

HTTP://WWW.DICTIONARY.COM

VOCABULARY WORDS. (PG. 166, 167)

ABOUT THE AUTHOR

Renée Wendinger

Renée Wendinger is from southern Minnesota and is the youngest of five children. She is a wife, mother, and grand-mother.

Renée's mother, Sophia (Kaminsky) Hillesheim, was one of the children of the orphan trains taking part in a phenomenal journey from New York City to the Midwest.

Inspired by her mother to write a history of the period and the children's experiences, Renée, an avid historian, has researched the premise for many years. This is her first book.

Renée is a speaker on the subject of the orphan trains and immigration experience offering a historical slide symposium to educators and schools, community and civic organizations, and libraries and historical centers.

She serves the Midwest Orphan Train Riders from New York Organization as president.

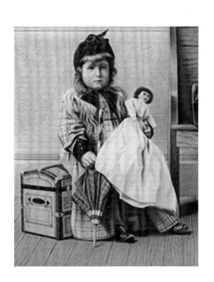

waiting for the train...